Start with Jesus

Other Books by Julianne Stanz

The Catechist's Backpack: Spiritual Essentials for the Journey
(with Joe Paprocki, D.Min.)

*Developing Disciples of Christ: Understanding the Critical Relationship
between Catechesis and Evangelization*

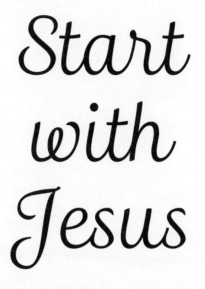

Start with Jesus

HOW EVERYDAY DISCIPLES WILL RENEW THE CHURCH

JULIANNE STANZ

LOYOLAPRESS.
A JESUIT MINISTRY
Chicago

LOYOLA PRESS.
A JESUIT MINISTRY

3441 N. Ashland Avenue
Chicago, Illinois 60657
(800) 621-1008
www.loyolapress.com

Scripture quotations contained herein are from the *New Revised Standard Version Bible: Catholic Edition*, copyright © 1993 and 1989 by the Division of Christian Education of the National Council of the Churches of Christ in the U.S.A. Used by permission. All rights reserved.

Cover art credit: imamember/iStock/Getty Images.

ISBN: 978-0-8294-4884-9
Library of Congress Control Number: 2019945719

Printed in the United States of America.
19 20 21 22 23 24 25 26 27 28 LSC 10 9 8 7 6 5 4 3 2 1

To my husband, Wayne, and our children, Ian, Ava, and Sean-Patrick. Is tu gra mo chroi!

Contents

Introduction: I Still Believe... ix

1 Reclaiming the Fire of Parish Life 1

2 What Is the Good News?.. 13

3 How Did Jesus Form Disciples? 27

4 The Parish That Prays Together Stays Together 41

5 Hope, Healing, and Hospitality: The Hinge Points
of Discipleship 53

6 The Art of Accompaniment... 67

7 Missionary Discipleship and Culture Change 81

8 Start with Who and Why... 93

9 From the Inside Out: Our People ARE the Program...... 107

10 Follow the Leader: Your Parish Process of Missionary
Discipleship 117

11 The Parish That Started with Jesus 133

12 It Also Starts with You!.. 145

Conclusion: Let's Get Moving for Jesus! 159

About the Author 162

And by my God I can leap over a wall.
—Psalm 18:29

Introduction: I Still Believe

"I came to bring fire to the earth, and how I wish it were already kindled!"

—Luke 12:49

For the past seventeen years, I have worked directly with and supported various parish ministries at the local, diocesan, and national level. I have worked as director of religious education, youth minister, adult faith formation director, young-adult minister, new evangelization director, and discipleship formation director. My work as a national speaker and a consultant to the United States Conference of Catholic Bishops (USCCB) Committee on Evangelization and Catechesis has given me a unique perspective on parish and diocesan life in the United States. So, too, has my generational reality: I just aged out of the millennial generation, the rare bird of Catholic parishes today (particularly in leadership), and I am also an immigrant. Currently, I serve on a parish council, lector regularly, and serve as the administrator of my parish social media page. When it comes to parish life, you can definitely say that I am "all in"!

Today, as I visit parishes across the country, signs of new life and growth are emerging in pockets of diocesan and parish life. However, the reality is that the majority of our Catholic parishes cannot even be said to be in maintenance anymore but in decline. And what of our people? Over and over, I hear from committed and engaged parishioners who love their faith and love their parishes and are tired and stretched too thin. Something has to change. We have to change. What once was the slow drip of decline in the Northeast and Midwest, for example, has now become a steady stream as our numbers dwindle and our parishes become quieter for lack of activity and human interaction. In the Southeast, many parishes are growing and some report that they need to consider new building projects but are afraid to do so, given the current reality of parish life. Some say that it is time to move beyond the current structure of parish life and start something new. Also, a good many say that nothing is wrong at all.

And yet, I still believe.

I still believe that the Catholic parish is the best nucleus to help people encounter and be nourished by Jesus Christ, to grow in friendship and solidarity with others, and to be the change that our local communities badly need. As communities of faith, parishes do not exist in the Catholic Church just for themselves but are given to the whole world as a source of salt and light (Matthew 5:13–14). The parish is meant to be a place where

- we are invited, welcomed, nurtured, and uplifted
- we belong to a family of faith where we are not just formed but transformed and then sent out to transform the world
- we are challenged to grow, to step outside our comfort zones, and to be sharpened as "iron sharpens iron" (Proverbs 27:17)
- we are called to enter the tomb of our own suffering and the suffering of others and reconcile it to the cross
- Good Friday gives way to Resurrection Sunday
- sinners are made into disciples and disciples are transformed into saints by living out the call to holiness

Modern Western culture is slowly crucifying Christians on the cross of subjectivity, individuality, and consumerism. But the Catholic Church continues to offer a compelling vision of what the human person is and can be—and a vision of how to grow in love for God and one another.

I believe that our Church is not just the medicine for the culture in which it lives but also the cure.

This cure comes about through the transformation of people who change and shape the world, using the model of Jesus' life with the disciples. Jesus took ordinary people, people the world at the time saw as being dispensable and unimportant, and turned them into the greatest saints the world has ever known. He transformed simple fishermen and traders into men and women who utterly altered the society in which they lived.

In our parishes, we, too, have the opportunity to transform people to change cultures and lives: people who are sent on mission. In our parishes, we have the privilege of walking with people through the most joyful and most difficult times of their lives. We grow together as people of faith, equipped with the skills we need to cope with daily life, while sharing our faith with the world credibly and authentically. Jesus didn't outsource his discipleship efforts to other leaders, and neither should we. While we can learn from the wisdom of others, there is no substitute for learning from Jesus.

Jesus waited until he had a well-formed core group that could model and replicate what he did for them. In our Catholic parishes, we are equipping the next generation of saints in our disciple-making efforts. Do you believe this is possible? You must, if you are reading this book.

There are many books on the problems facing the Catholic Church. This is not one of them. There are also books about ideas that can help your parish grow. This book will incorporate new ideas, but it is not a checklist of small tweaks your parish might benefit from. There are other books that define discipleship but do not give an action plan for how to foster a culture of discipleship.

This is a book that seeks to help you understand why our parishes must be transformed from the inside out as our people are equipped to bring the gospel to their families, neighborhoods, and communities. It is a book less about programs and checklists than about process, people, and culture. This is a book that starts with Jesus, what he did, and what he asked us to do. It is a book that takes seriously Pope Francis's charge to become missionary disciples and outlines a process that parishes can integrate into their efforts to become centers of missionary outreach in the spirit of the new evangelization. It is a book that challenges each of us to grow as a disciple so that we can become a disciple maker and accompany others on the way. Whether you are a regular "person in the pew," a volunteer at your parish, or a paid parish minister, you are a leader for the Catholic Church.

Many times, our approach to parish life is like baking a cake. We take a recipe that has worked in another parish and try to follow it exactly, hoping it will translate to our own parish. But our ingredients are different because our parishes and our people are different. Can we learn from other Catholic parishes and, indeed, other Christian parishes? You bet! But following a cake recipe is precise, with little room for flexibility, adaptability, and creativity. In my experience, parish life is more like a rich stew of people, cultures, subcultures, and communities that gather every week. As long as you have some basic ingredients on hand and you understand how Jesus formed disciples, your stew will be flavorful and hearty and can adapt to the seasons with some changes here and there.

While indicators of a parish's success often focus on the externals (the institution), this book focuses on the internal (the people longing for God who have the capacity to set the world on fire). It sets forth a vision for a rich stew of missionary discipleship in the parish. It offers practical ways by which your parish can release the fire of your people to become a community of missionary disciples that makes an impact on the wider community.

This book outlines a vision for every parish—large or small, urban or rural. This vision does not require a celebrity pastor or a high-powered parish team. Ordinary parishes can become extraordinary by tapping into their best resource: their people. Every Catholic parish has something incredible to offer the world: the presence of Jesus Christ and the people who love him.

Reclaiming the Fire of Parish Life

In all my years of experience, the moment that transformed how I look at parish life came through the wisdom of my three-year-old son, Ian. It was a Sunday morning when I went to wake him up. "What day is it?" he asked sleepily. "It's Sunday, son. That means it's time for church," I said. Under the blankets I heard an audible sigh of displeasure. And then he said the words that all parents dread: "I don't want to go to Mass." It was the first time I had ever heard him say this, and so I asked him why. In my mind, I thought about all the reasons a child might not want to go to Mass: how few children he would see in our church again that weekend; the quietness and lack of movement; the fact that he often cannot see what is happening; the music; the lack of snacks; and so on. But my son did not list one of those reasons, as I expected. "I don't want to go to church, Mama," he whispered, "because nobody looks happy there."

I thought my heart was going to break.

Nobody Looks Happy There

What do our children see when they look at our parishes? What do they experience? What do they see in each of us? In me? I thought about what my children saw on a Sunday morning in our home. Was I calm and filled with expectant joy about going to Mass? Or was I the harried mom stretched for time who rushed my children out the door and into a pew without thinking? Were we prepared as a family for the gift of the Eucharist? The answer was no. If we want our children to become joyful witnesses to their faith, they must see it first in us as parents. If we want our parishes to be places of joy and transformation, then we must see it first in our parishioners.

Our parishes must reclaim the fire and excitement for faith so that it is visible to all, especially to the least among us. This is especially true and critical for active parishioners and the parish team. If your committed parishioners do not radiate love for their faith, don't expect those they encounter to radiate joy either.

Our parishes are complex systems, communities within communities that work together, but, essentially, they are composed of people. It is our people who will renew our parishes, not programs, slick marketing, or great resources. Those factors are peripheral to the core work of renewing our parishes by renewing our people, beginning with our own disposition and witness. Throughout the book, you will notice that I refer to "parish leaders" and "leaders in the parish." Is there a difference? Yes, there is. The term "parish leaders" refers to those in formal ministerial roles, including the pastor and paid parish staff. These are the people who most often compose a parish staff or team. "Leaders in the parish" refers to members of the parish who have the gifts or the potential to help others grow in their faith and, with them, the parish. This includes volunteers, committee members, and all those who want to contribute to leading the Church they love. If we are going to renew our parishes, we need all people to step up and be leaders, working with our parish leaders to shape the parish and the community in which it lives. Together, we must recover the sense of fire and energy that comes from a faith fully alive and in touch with the Holy Spirit.

Go Set the World on Fire!

Fire has played one of the most significant roles in the advancement of civilization. The world depends on the warmth and energy of the biggest fire near the Earth—the sun. Without fire, there would be no life. Fire and life go hand in hand.

This is also true of our spiritual lives. The metaphor of fire is used throughout the Bible to indicate the presence of God directly and the presence of God in others. God is described as a "consuming fire" (Hebrews 12:29), and we are told that we will be baptized with the Holy Spirit and fire (Matthew 3:11). Without the fire of our faith, we would be lifeless Christians lacking fervor and energy. We would have no "get up and go"!

Too often, our approach to our faith lacks the fire or energy that it deserves. Too often, what once was an energetic fire dies down to a few burning embers as we get stuck in comfortable and familiar patterns. Does the fire of our faith produce change in ourselves and in others? Does it inspire and energize? Does our parish reflect a fire that is warming, moving, and inviting? Or has our fire died down so that it is barely visible? Fire can be a creative or a destructive force; it is never static but constantly moving, growing, and consuming. And yet, many parishes have become stuck in outdated modes and methods that hold them back from unleashing the energy and warmth of the gospel fire reflected in our people.

Much as a fire will die out or a circuit will short when it reaches maximum overload, we as a Church have reached what Pope Francis calls "a diagnostic overload" (*Evangelii Gaudium*, #50). This overload, caused by a flurry of activity coupled with dwindling personnel and financial resources, can smother the fire of parish life. If we put more and more activities, events, programs, and stresses on our parishes, we risk allowing our fires to dwindle to bare embers.

This danger can be avoided, Pope Francis reminds us, only by an evangelical discernment that prioritizes missionary discipleship. This requires a change from a more administrative model of ministry to an evangelical missionary model that emphasizes transformation of the parish culture through relationship building, accompaniment, and community impact.

Fire is visible and always produces change, energy, and focus. St. Ignatius of Loyola urged his followers to go set the world on fire, and there is no better place to do this than in the parish. The parish is ordinarily the first point of contact for most Catholics, particularly those who have been away from the Church and who seek to return home. In the parish, we become engaged with the wider Church community, are nourished by Scripture and the sacraments, and have opportunities for initial and ongoing formation in faith.

And, in our parishes there are many overlooked leaders waiting for someone to notice them and invite them into a deeper relationship with the Lord. In fact, you as a reader of this book might be an unrealized leader with tremendous potential to help our parishes share the gospel. If you are waiting for a sign, this is it! Do not be afraid to see yourself as a leader in your parish and your Church; Jesus Christ himself is depending on it! We, as leaders in our parishes, must be equipped to see how every aspect of life is an opportunity to go out into the world and make disciples of all peoples (Matthew 28:19), remembering that it is primarily in the parish that God's people are brought to new birth through water and the Spirit (John 3:5) and to eternal life in the body and blood of his Son (John 6:54). Each of us is asked to bring to others the good news of the gospel and share how it has transformed our lives. This is what God wants for each of us, and it is the deepest identity of the Church: bringing the Good News to others.

Our Deepest Identity

The word *evangelize* comes from the Greek word "to bring the Good News." Pope Paul VI made it clear, in his encyclical *Evangelii Nuntiandi*, that the Church "exists in order to evangelize" (#14). Evangelization is the "deepest identity" of the Church. While it may seem paradoxical to refer to the Catholic Church as "evangelical," the DNA of Catholicism is evangelization: the mandate to evangelize comes from Jesus Christ himself. Jesus commanded us to "Go therefore and make disciples of all nations, baptizing them in the name of the Father and of the Son and of the Holy Spirit, and teaching them to obey everything that I have commanded you" (Matthew 28:19–20). Jesus is the center of evangelization, the heart of catechesis, and the fire of parish life. We share not just the message of Christ but also his very person. Jesus *is* the Good News.

Why did Christ want us to share him and his message with the world? Jesus' mission was to bring all to his father, God the Father, who is our Father. Jesus accomplishes his Father's work: the salvation of all by his redemptive suffering, death, and Resurrection. Jesus is "the message, the messenger, the purpose of his message, and the consummation of the message" (*National Directory for Catechesis*, 4). The commission to baptize using the formula of Father, Son, and Holy Spirit incorporates all Christians into Trinitarian love. This love is the fountain of love for everyone who chooses to accept it. It is our responsibility to share Jesus and his message with those in our families, neighborhoods, and wider communities. This is our deepest identity and our mission. So, where might you start? In your home? In your parish? In your community? The answer is all three. Let's take a look.

Jerusalem, Judea, and Samaria

"But you will receive power when the Holy Spirit has come upon you; and you will be my witnesses in Jerusalem, in all Judea and Samaria, and to the ends of the earth."

—Acts 1:8

In a sense, Jesus' last words are his last will and testament. He tells us, his disciples, that power will come to us when we receive the Holy Spirit, so that we can be his witnesses to the ends of the earth. He leaves us with specific directions about where we should be witnesses: Jerusalem, Judea, and Samaria. Why these three places?

Jerusalem, as the most holy and sacred place, represents our home, or the center of the Church's activities as the "domestic church." This is where we start: at home and in our parish. Next, Jesus names Judea. Judea was the region in which Jerusalem was located. So, after beginning at home, we are called to go out into our neighborhoods to spread the Good News. Lastly, Jesus asks us to go to Samaria. The Jews avoided Samaria and saw the Samaritans as outcasts who were not to be trusted. Jesus asks us to go out from what is most familiar and comfortable to be with those who are marginalized.

Our parishes naturally lead us outward from Jerusalem to Judea and Samaria as we encounter children and adults from all backgrounds, faith journeys, and cultures. We begin in our homes and parishes with those who are registered and those who are not registered, those who come to Mass regularly and those who come once or twice a year. We begin with those who have "ears to hear" (Matthew 11:15) and help them grow in faith so that they in turn can share their faith in their homes, neighborhoods, and schools.

Our parish teams know certain facets of parish life; they have close contact with some parishioners—often the ones who are the most active in ministries—and pay less attention to those they do not know as well. This is not because of any malicious intent. It is a case of "not knowing whom we do not know." But if we do not know our people and their potential, we will not be able to unleash their inner fire for the work of the kingdom. As a result, our parish fire will not burn as strongly or as brightly.

Our parishioners can help identify those we need to reach more effectively by working together with the parish team. Our parish teams cannot reach everyone, but they can with your help. It is time for each of us to become, in the words of Pope Francis, a "missionary disciple." Now, you might be a bit nervous about the term "missionary disciple" if you are hearing it for the first time or if you have heard it before but are not sure what it means. But let me reassure you, the concept is at the core of who we are as Catholics: our mission is to evangelize and share our faith with others, right where we are—especially where we are. Let's look at this more closely, starting with a question you might be asking.

Isn't Being a Missionary Only for Those Who Go to Remote Places?

In the past, evangelization focused on those who had never heard of Christ and his teachings. The mission field was seen as foreign, not domestic. "Sending money overseas to little pagan babies" was how my neighbor described missionary activity from that era of the Church. Many Catholics born before the Second Vatican Council remember the plea for money to be sent overseas to the foreign missions. Throughout the last century, the work of evangelization and mission was increasingly seen as the purview of a select group of people: those who were called missionaries. This absolved many Catholics of the commission to make disciples. The imperative to evangelize was confined to a professional class of people who worked for the Church rather than to the average person in the pew.

Catholicism still carries within it the vestiges of a historical memory where Catholics in America were set apart because of their beliefs and were often viewed with outright suspicion and hostility. Catholics lived together in small, tight-knit communities—the Irish on the South side of Chicago or the Polish or Italian communities in New York City, for example—communities where faith was at the heart of their lives. During this time, there were many horror stories of how Catholic immigrants were treated, and as a result, many Catholics bought into the lie that faith was to be kept private and not to be shared in the public square. A consequence of this mistreatment was that Catholics cultivated a strong desire to "blend in" as they became increasingly unwilling to draw attention to themselves and their faith, thus leading to an erosion of faith in the public square. Think, for example, about how many times you may have heard Catholics say, "The Church should not comment on politics." Many believe that the Church should offer no public commentary on the poor, on the misuse of resources, on systems that oppress others, on technological advancement, on science—the list goes on and on. Of course, this goes against the core of the gospel message. This dichotomy between faith and life was referenced by the Fathers of the Second Vatican Council in *Gaudium et Spes*, #43, when they wrote: "This split between the faith which many profess, and their daily lives, deserves to be counted among the more serious errors of our age."

While faith is certainly personal, it is not meant to be a private matter. If we are going to reclaim the fire of parish life, we must get over our fear of evangelizing and begin to evangelize by sharing our faith with others in our own unique way. We become an evangelizing Church by becoming who we are intended to be as a Church: the body of Christ. All that we say and do should have at its source the Good News of the message and person of Jesus Christ, who wants to bring us all home to his Father through the power of the Holy Spirit.

So how do we, the Church, evangelize?

Evangelization aims at transforming hearts (interior change) and the world (external change). Too often, people think that door-to-door conversations and preaching from street corners are the only ways we can evangelize. But there are many ways that we, as Catholics, can evangelize. In *Evangelii Nuntiandi*, Pope Paul VI writes that evangelization includes the following:

- catechesis
- preaching
- liturgy
- sacraments
- popular piety
- witness of the Christian life
- mass media
- personal contact

It is important to remember that, while we are all called to evangelize, the Holy Spirit is the actual agent of evangelization. We are the instruments called to evangelize and to be evangelized, but it is always the grace of the Holy Spirit that fuels the conversion. This is a nuance that often gets missed. God is present in every life, whether we recognize it or not. He is present in those who are in our parishes and those who are not, those who pray with us and those who do not, those who think as we do and those who do not. In all our interactions with others, we can bring Christ to them, but we can also acknowledge Jesus, who already dwells in their hearts and who is a gift to us too. It is a gift of giving and receiving. But, to do this, we need to make sure that we are growing in our friendship with Jesus Christ and his Body, the Church.

Undoubtedly, one of the central calls for us at this time is to develop a deep and abiding relationship with Jesus Christ through the power of the Holy Spirit that transforms us from the inside out. Right now, you might be struggling with where to begin or how to begin. You might even wonder if this approach is Catholic. Let me reassure you that it is. So, let's get back to basics by focusing on our roots and the central message of our faith.

_____ TAKING ACTION _____

Pray as You Go (and Make Disciples)

Prayer for the New Evangelization

God, our Father, I pray that through the Holy Spirit I might hear the call of the New Evangelization to deepen my faith, grow in confidence to proclaim the Gospel and boldly witness to the saving grace of your Son, Jesus Christ, who lives and reigns with you, in the unity of the Holy Spirit, one God, for ever and ever. Amen.

—adapted from the *Prayer for the New Evangelization*, USCCB

Personal Principle

I invite Christians, everywhere, at this very moment, to a renewed personal encounter with Jesus Christ, or at least an openness to letting him encounter them; I ask all of you to do this unfailingly each day.

—*Evangelii Gaudium*, #3

It is important that we speak not just about Jesus but to Jesus. Outside of the Sunday obligation to attend Mass, many Catholics are not comfortable speaking about Jesus or are unsure how to speak to Jesus. We might be more comfortable speaking about God than about his Son, Jesus, and we rarely mention the Holy Spirit. This change starts with each one of us. We might be uncomfortable speaking about our faith, but it is something that we must do.

Start with the following questions:

When I pray, which member of the Holy Trinity do I pray most with? Why? How do I speak to and listen to Jesus, individually and with others? Is the name of Jesus on my lips? Is our parish a place filled with people who love Jesus?

The chapter 1 online printable resource, "Everyday Evangelization," outlines some simple ways you can strengthen your faith so that you can share the Good News with others. www.loyolapress.com/startwithjesus

Parish Priority

> The effort of the new evangelization faces two dangers: one is inertia, laziness, not doing anything and letting others do all the work; the other is launching into many busy but ultimately empty, human activities.
>
> —Raniero Cantalamessa, OFM Cap, *Navigating the New Evangelization* (Pauline Books, 2014, 24)

There are many ways for us to encounter Christ individually but also as a parish team.

Set aside some time to encounter Christ. This could be at a set time: praying a mealtime prayer alone or with others or spending time in morning prayer. If you are part of a parish team and have a PA system, consider having chimes play at certain hours such as twelve o'clock for the Angelus or three o'clock for the Divine Mercy. Other suggestions include reading Scripture or performing a spiritual or corporal act of mercy. Pray that God will help you recognize unexpected encounters with Christ in every opportunity.

You can use the chapter 1 online printable resource, "Everyday Evangelization in the Parish Office," to structure your reflection. www.loyolapress.com/startwithjesus

2

What Is the Good News?

It was a day I will never forget. Late one afternoon while I was working as a high school counselor, one of my students, John, walked into my office and told me that he had tried to take his life earlier that day but failed. Breaking down in tears, he shared with me how he was being bullied and harassed by those who were making his life "a living hell." It was a heartbreaking situation. After some representatives of the school met with John and his parents, we worked on a care plan from multiple angles, including addressing John's mental, emotional, and physical health.

After this meeting, John asked me if we could meet daily to talk about his faith, and, of course, I agreed. He felt that he needed the support of someone to walk with him while he figured out "some things." During these conversations, he shared with me the deepest longings of his heart and his desire to grow in faith and in self-confidence. Some weeks later, I gave John a prayer card that had become meaningful to me and that I thought he would appreciate. On the back of the card was the Serenity Prayer, and on the front was the image by Andrea Mantegna titled *Christ's Descent into Limbo*. Christ bends toward a man emerging from the depths of hell. His face and hands are turned toward Christ. John was drawn to this profound and emotional image and asked why I had chosen it for him.

I explained to John that during the Apostles' Creed, we say the words "he descended into hell" and "on the third day he rose again from the dead." These words can seem peculiar when we take the time to deeply reflect on them. Christ descended into the abode of the dead, but why?

Scripture calls the abode of the dead, to which Christ descended, "hell" or *Sheol* in Hebrew or *Hades* in Greek. The *Catechism of the Catholic Church* reminds us that "Jesus did not descend into hell to deliver the damned, nor to destroy the hell of damnation, but to free the just who had gone before him" (*CCC*, #633). Mantegna's image represents the journey that Jesus made into the depths of hell to preach the gospel to the "spirits in prison" (1 Peter 3:19). The word *prison* in this context (Greek, *Phulake*) refers to the place where the departed souls rest prior to Jesus' opening the gates of heaven. This transitory place is known as limbo. The *Catechism* further explains that "he descended there as Savior, proclaiming the Good News to the spirits imprisoned there" (*CCC*, #632).

Think about that! The Good News was preached even to the dead. Jesus himself illuminated the darkness of death, despair, hopelessness, and hell. He came to share the message of the gospel with those in hell so that they would hear the voice of the Son of God and have life. By the expression "he descended into hell," we confess that Jesus has conquered death and hell to bring us to new life. I gave John this prayer card precisely for this reason. There is no place of torment, no state of fear, no realm of terror where you can go where Christ has not walked before you. Christ walks at your side no matter what hell you find yourself in. I explained to John that, while he was in the midst of what he called a living hell, Christ never abandoned him but was walking beside him and carrying him through it. From that moment on, John said that he knew that he was never alone because Christ was always with him and gave him the strength and comfort to face each day.

Years later I happened to run into John, and he pulled from his wallet the card I had given him. The message that Christ was with him in every moment of his life had become a catalyst for his growth in faith. Over the years I came to recognize that I had shared a significant piece of the core gospel message with John without knowing it. This message is at the heart of our faith and is formally known as the *kerygma*. Now, before we unpack what this means, I want to add a small caveat. The term "kerygma" is considered to be what we would call "insider language," meaning that it is meant for leaders or highly engaged parishioners only. It is quite likely that the term is intimidating for those in an early stage of their faith development, those with a tenuous affiliation to Catholicism, and those who are disaffiliated from the Catholic Church. While it is important that we as leaders know and understand the core gospel message and its application, advertising or marketing events at the parish as "kerygma events" will likely be off-putting and not attract your desired audience.

Getting to the Core

Kerygma, meaning "proclamation," comes from the Greek word *kerusso*, meaning "herald," or one who proclaims. As the apostles began sharing their experience of Jesus Christ, they started with the basics of his life, death, and Resurrection—through Jesus, God had drawn near to his people. Gradually, and only after people understood and accepted the basic message, did they progress to a much fuller instruction or teaching (*didache*) in the faith. In the early Church, quite a bit of time was devoted to initial proclamation, helping people develop a relationship with the Person of the Good News. In this way, Jesus is both the message and the messenger.

Today, many have not heard the Good News or may have heard bits and pieces of the Christian story but have not accepted it fully. They seem to get lost in the labyrinthine complexity of the teachings and doctrines of the Church and, to use a popular expression, "miss the forest for the trees." A back-to-basics approach is needed now more than ever to help people discover, recover, or uncover their belief in the core tenets of our faith: the life, death, and Resurrection of Jesus.

From the lips of the apostles, the splendid simplicity of this central message was boldly proclaimed to different audiences in ways that were tailored to their receptivity, their background, and their standing in the community. We, too, are called to proclaim the Good News, as the disciples did, with courage and conviction. Even though the term *kerygma* might be new to us, we as Catholics are immersed in the proclamation of the Good News regularly. For instance, in the Creed we proclaim at Mass, we summarize the core of the kerygma:

> For us men and for our salvation he came down from heaven: and by the Holy Spirit was incarnate of the Virgin Mary, and was made man.
>
> For our sake he was crucified under Pontius Pilate; he suffered death and was buried. On the third day he rose again in accordance with the Scriptures; he ascended into heaven and is seated at the right hand of the Father.

As it did with my student John, this message of the saving power of Jesus transforms us and moves us to conversion and ongoing conversion. This Good News is the most freeing and life-giving news we can hear. The Good News is what liberates us and helps us become more deeply conformed to Christ.

The Good News Is GOOD News!

I remember the day my sister told me that she was expecting her first baby. I wrapped her in a hug and squeezed her so hard she was breathless. My sister was going to have a child, and I would be an aunt! Shout it from the rooftops! Once she had given permission to share the news publicly, I couldn't wait to tell all my friends. And that's what I did—I told all my friends, some two or three times in my excitement and joy for this new child.

Every Sunday at Mass, we hear Good News. And what is our response to this Good News? The priest or deacon says, "The Gospel of the Lord," and we respond, "Praise to you, Lord Jesus Christ." Now I want you to think about the tone we use to say, "Praise to you, Lord Jesus Christ." Can you hear the sound? It's probably the understated and vague muffle of a lukewarm Catholic response.

In the Gospels, we hear *Good* News. That's right, Good News. I don't know anyone who responds to good news with a sleepy mumble and a yawn! The Cubs win the World Series! Your friend passes an important exam! Your spouse gets a clean bill of health after a scare! Can you feel the excitement? The joy? The desire to run out and share your good news with everybody? Yes, these are natural responses that should characterize our hearing of good news.

Good news is called that for a reason. When we hear the Word of God and say, "Praise to you, Lord Jesus Christ," we should be filled with a joy so contagious that it affects and infects others. In *Under the Influence of Jesus: The Transforming Experience of Encountering Christ* (Chicago: Loyola Press, 2014), Joe Paprocki reminds us that "ultimately, the goal of discipleship is contagion: 'infecting' others with the Good News through our words and actions" (139). This proclamation of Good News must be situated at the heart of our lives as Catholics and imbedded in every single parish event, experience, and ministry—every single one. Every activity in the parish should point more deeply to Jesus. If it does not, then we must abandon it because it does not serve the mission. Becoming familiar with the kerygma is essential to us all but especially to our parish teams so that it can be woven into the tapestry of parish life.

Recipe Basics

If the kerygma is to be imbedded in all our efforts, what is the best formula to use? The short answer is that there isn't a foolproof recipe that can be replicated exactly. We are not going back to a Baltimore Catechism methodology where we regurgitate statements without integrating them or assimilating them. The architecture of the kerygma depends on the audience and the receptivity of the hearer. In the Scriptures, the disciples speak Good News in different ways and at different times, but the core message is always the same. Yet, in its most basic form, the kerygma contains five essential movements: creation, fall, redemption, salvation, and re-creation.

- **Creation.** A loving God created the world, and each of us is created to be in relationship with him.
- **Fall.** Through humanity, sin entered the world, and our perfect union with God was broken.
- **Redemption.** God sent his beloved Son, Jesus, to redeem humanity. Jesus' life, death, and Resurrection atone for the sins of the world. We are offered a share in this redemption.
- **Salvation.** Belief in Jesus Christ and the Father who sent him is necessary in order to be saved.
- **Re-creation.** From his position as Messiah, Jesus rules all things, and we are created anew through his life, death, Resurrection, and Ascension. The presence of the Holy Spirit is a gift of the Father to his beloved children.

Most Catholics have some idea of the basic gospel story but need to hear the basics many times for it to take root. Some might be familiar with one of the movements but not all of them. Some people will need a slightly different or longer version of the message, such as "the Great Story" in nine acts presented by Sherry Weddell in her book *Forming Intentional Disciples: The Path to Knowing and Following Jesus.*

- **The Kingdom:** an invitation to live in a reality in which God's will reigns
- **Jesus, Face of the Kingdom:** an invitation to know the Person who embodies the kingdom
- **Jesus, the Kingdom in Word and Deed:** the work of the kingdom—healing, forgiving, proclaiming, and teaching
- **Jesus Embraces the Cross:** the mystery of dying as the key to eternal life
- **Resurrection, Ascension, New Life, Adoption, and the Kingdom:** the victory over sin and death
- **Jesus Asks Me to Follow Him:** an invitation to adopt this new way of living known as discipleship
- **Personal Sin and Forgiveness:** transformation of the way we live
- **Dropping the Net:** making a firm commitment to Christ and his body, the Church
- **The Life of Discipleship:** waking up each day to a new way of living

Regardless of the format you use, it is important for you to be thoroughly familiar with the core message before you introduce it to others. In addition to your own familiarity, the following are some important considerations to keep in mind.

Construct wisely. The architecture of the kerygma depends on the audience, the maturity, and the degree of receptivity of the hearers. Spend time thinking about which movement of the kerygma the person(s) might be familiar or unfamiliar with and what their response to the story has been up to this point.

It is what it is. Proclamation is proclamation. It is not intended to be full catechesis, nor is its goal to get someone to "come back to Mass." Allow the power of the basic gospel story to touch the person's heart without unnecessary explanation.

K.I.S.S. Keep It Simple, Sweetie. Unless absolutely necessary, avoid lengthy exegesis and commentary. Introduce the kerygma using simple but powerful statements.

Watch terminology. We have a whole host of terms that we use in the Catholic Church that can be off-putting or confusing. Say what you mean and mean what you say. Define terms such as Resurrection and Ascension. Don't assume the person knows what these terms mean.

Easy does it. If you sense that your audience is switching off, take a break and come back to this discussion again later.

Pray. Begin your presentation of the gospel story with prayer. Prayer before, during, and after the process is not optional.

Reflect and repeat. The average person needs to hear the gospel story more than once so that he or she can grasp the significance of the message, reflect on it, and internalize it. Repeat the message in different ways at different times.

Be patiently pastoral. Making a conscious decision to follow Jesus can be a painful experience for some people. It's critical that we are patient and loving during the process.

Touch base. Don't leave people hanging. Follow up later with a conversation, and clarify or go deeper.

The Challenge: Make it Personal

Now if Christ is proclaimed as raised from the dead, how can some of you say there is no resurrection of the dead? If there is no resurrection of the dead, then Christ has not been raised; and if Christ has not been raised, then our proclamation has been in vain and your faith has been in vain.

—1 Corinthian 15:12–14

Personalizing the gospel message can be a powerful experience. It moves us from seeing the gospel as something that happened outside of ourselves to seeing it as something we participate in. The following format may help people personally connect to the Gospel story:

- A loving God created me for relationship with him.
- I have broken my relationship with God through my sin.
- Jesus restores my relationship with God through his life, death, and Resurrection.
- Jesus invites me to trust him, to turn from sin, and to give my life to him.
- Jesus has poured the Holy Spirit into my heart to bring me to new life in his Church and sends his Church on a mission so that others can experience that new life.

I have presented this basic gospel story in a ten-minute conversation and over a daylong retreat. Once you are familiar with the movements, you can adapt it as necessary. A helpful image is one drawn from St. Catherine of Siena's "A Treatise of Divine Providence," part 1 of her *Dialogue*. She uses the metaphor of a bridge to describe our relationship with God. Christ is the bridge that unites us to God across the chasm of sin, which she portrays as a raging river that tries to carry us away. The bridge represents our crossing from the darkness of sin to the light of Christ. We must reclaim the ability to speak the core message into our lives and all our parish structures, activities, and processes. Try to get past the resistance that we "know this stuff" so that we do not become inoculated to its power in our own lives and in the lives of others.

The chapter 2 online printable, "Back to Basics: Encountering Jesus," provides an overview of what the framework for the core gospel message could look like for you. www.loyolapress.com/startwithjesus

The call to missionary discipleship is not about changing behavior or getting people to join a parish. Instead, it is about affecting conversion in the life of every person we encounter and walking with him or her on the journey to Christ. Joining a parish comes later—often much later—for many people. Conversion, or *metanoia*, involves a sincere transformation of mind and heart to Christ. It means turning away from one thing in order to turn toward something else. The *Catechism of the Catholic Church* outlines two conversions that happen in a person's life.

1. The first and most fundamental conversion happens during the Sacrament of Baptism (#1427). Baptismal profession is the foundation of our spiritual house.

2. The second conversion happens throughout our lives and is a task for the whole Church to facilitate. St. Peter's conversion after his denial of Christ is an example of this kind of conversion (#1428–1429). This conversion may be a "wow" moment or a series of smaller movements over time.

Conversion is difficult and often painful. St. Peter wept openly at his denial of Christ. At a conference I once attended, I met a lady named Shirley who summed up the kerygma through three major movements in her life: her life before she had a relationship with Christ and was living in a way not in harmony with the gospel; her life during a time of great suffering as a result of her choices when she felt the love and mercy of God touch her heart; and her life afterward. She summed up her story as follows: "I was (a mess). God did (what he did). I am (a new woman!)" Then she sat down. It was succinct, authentic, and powerful.

The Heart That Matters

The expression "An arrow that is aimed at the head will not pierce the heart" helps us understand the intimate relationship between falling in love with Christ and learning more about him, what we in the Church call evangelization and catechesis. The kerygma is the arrow that pierces the heart of the seeker of Christ. Without the core message, our teaching will not be effective or bear fruit. Pope Francis reminds us that on our lips "the first proclamation must ring out over and over: 'Jesus Christ loves you; he gave his life to save you; and now he is living at your side every day to enlighten, strengthen and free you'" (*Evangelii Gaudium*, #164).

A faithful witness coupled with basic proclamation is the best catalyst for growth in the spiritual life. There is a tendency to think that initial proclamation is deficient because it is too basic. This is not the case. The Good News ought to elicit a response, over time transforming the hearer of the Word into a proclaimer of the Word and, finally, into a doer of the Word. As such, this message should constitute the centerpiece of our lives as Christians and as parish communities. When people say, "Let's get to the heart of the matter," what they mean is that they want to go straight to the core and, once there, find that it is the heart that matters most of all. All else is peripheral.

—————————— **TAKING ACTION** ————————

Pray as You Go (and Make Disciples)

Jesus,
We know that you are with us, and we feel your loving
     presence;
We call upon you to help us grow in friendship with you;
Help us share you with others;
We know that the work is difficult and hard.
May we see with clarity,
Regard all with charity,
And respond with alacrity.
In your name,
Amen

Personal Principle

The Good News, or the basic story of our salvation, ought to be at the heart of our lives. Set aside some time to pray through and reflect on the movements of the kerygma. It is important to note any areas where there is resistance. Pay attention to the places where you personally feel that you know the story and find it boring or trite. Reflecting on the kerygma often moves us from our heads to our hearts as we connect on a deeper level. God often uses our weaknesses or resistance to expose areas where growth is needed. Practice sharing the basic gospel story in your own words. Write down a couple of points. Next, think about someone who might not be familiar with the kerygma. How might you speak the kerygma to this person? Where would you start?

You can use the chapter 2 online printable resource, "Back to Basics: Encountering Jesus," to structure your reflection.
www.loyolapress.com/startwithjesus

Parish Priority

The *kerygma* is not simply a stage, but [the recurring theme] of a process that culminates in the maturity of the disciple of Jesus Christ. Without the *kerygma*, the other aspects of this process are condemned to sterility, with hearts not truly converted to the Lord. Only out of the *kerygma* does the possibility of a true Christian initiation occur. Hence, the Church should have it present in all its actions.

—Aparecida Document, #278a

Take out your parish calendar for the upcoming month and write down every activity, including Mass, faith formation, sacramental preparation, and small faith-sharing studies.

Divide every activity into three categories:

1. Opportunities to share the kerygma
2. Few-to-no opportunities to share the kerygma
3. Possible opportunities to share the kerygma

Group the activities as above and reflect on how the kerygma can be woven into every activity of the parish. Examine the list of those in the "no" category and make a decision to pause those activities at this time. Look at the other two categories and decide which activities should receive immediate priority and which can be tackled later.

You can use the chapter 2 online printable resource, "Back to Basics: Encountering Jesus," to structure your reflection.
www.loyolapress.com/startwithjesus

3

How Did Jesus Form Disciples?

In a series of essays entitled "What's Wrong with the World," written in 1910 by G. K. Chesterton, he states, "The Christian ideal has not been tried and found wanting. It has been found difficult; and left untried." He could have written those same words today, which is why we need more than ever to get back to the method modeled by the master, Jesus Christ. This method has worked across all ages, generations, and cultures. So, let's look at what discipleship is and how Jesus formed disciples.

What Is a Disciple?

The word *disciple* comes from the Greek word *mathetes*, meaning a pupil or student of the master. The master is, of course, Jesus Christ. A disciple is one who follows Jesus, loves him, desires to learn from him, to be with him, and to share him with others. The identity of a disciple springs from Jesus Christ, through faith and baptism, and grows in the Church, the community where all its members acquire equal dignity and participate in various ministries and gifts. We are disciples of a person, and that person is Jesus Christ. "Discipleship is not about achieving a height of holiness," remarks Kristin Bird, executive director of the Burning Hearts Apostolate, "but rather a depth of relationship that holiness flows from."

So, where do we begin in our discipleship efforts? We begin by starting with ourselves and our own conversion—and continued conversion—to Jesus Christ. At the USCCB General Assembly meeting in 2012, Cardinal Timothy Dolan challenged the bishops with the following words: "First things first. . . . We cannot engage culture unless we let [Jesus] first engage us; we cannot dialogue with others unless we first dialogue with Him; we cannot challenge others unless we first let Him challenge us."

We cannot lead others to Jesus until we ourselves have entered relationship with him. We ought not to evangelize others unless we have been evangelized, and we cannot disciple others effectively unless we are disciples. Every one of us, regardless of vocation, role in life, or ministry, is called to holiness and to growth in the Catholic faith. You might be wondering if you have the necessary qualifications for discipleship; well, you do! Your qualification comes from the Sacrament of Baptism, which is the core catalyst for the disciple's life. Baptism imparts to us the grace necessary to share the Gospel, and there are some keys that continue to help us grow as disciples. Below are what I call my ten Ds of discipleship.

The Ten Ds of Discipleship

1. **Desire.** We began our journey as a disciple in baptism but must also continually affirm our desire to grow in relationship with Jesus and his body the Church. Without this desire, we can become disconnected and apathetic.

2. **Discernment.** Being a disciple means that we must make the time to reflect on our lives. Just as Jesus went away to pray and discern whom to choose as his disciples, we must also discern what it means to be a disciple and grow in love for him. Discernment and prayer are at the heart of the disciple's life.

3. **Decision.** At some point in our lives, we recognize more fully that we need to set aside those distractions and habits that lead us away from Christ. This decision or series of decisions to say no to the things of the world and yes to Jesus Christ is at the heart of our ongoing conversion.

4. **Discipline.** Saying yes to Christ involves personal sacrifice and discipline. Time is the currency of discipleship, and if we want to grow as disciples, we must be disciplined in spending time with Christ and learning from him.

5. **Dwelling in the Word.** The Word of God holds the power to form and transform us. God speaks to us in his Word. Therefore, a disciple cannot grow and be nourished apart from the Word of God. Dwelling in the Word of God is absolutely essential for growth in the Christian life.

6. **Dependence on the Holy Spirit.** All the good that we do in life depends on the action or animation of the Holy Spirit. It is the Holy Spirit who shines through us and awakens in us the desire to follow Jesus and to grow in holiness. We must become more dependent on listening to the promptings and "nudgings" of the Holy Spirit.

7. **Denial.** Saying yes to God means saying no to those habits, beliefs, and practices that pull us away from him. Denial of self so that we can carry the cross helps us develop reliance on God and resilience for the journey ahead. Jesus reminds us that "if any want to become my followers, let them deny themselves and take up their cross and follow me" (Mark 8:34).

8. **Dedication.** Being a friend and follower of Jesus involves daily dedication to living a virtuous and moral life. Dedication involves sacrificing our time and self to give to others and to sanctify the world.

9. **Deliberation.** Intentionality is necessary for the disciple. Like all practices, growth in discipleship is the result of small daily actions that help us conform ourselves even more to Christ. This is not happenstance but, rather, takes time and effort to plan and center our lives around our relationship with Christ. In the words of John, "he must increase, but I must decrease" (John 3:30).

10. **Doing.** Discipleship is not a program but a process, a way of life. The entire discipleship process is an apprenticeship in faith, in the living out of the Christian life. We must move from being hearers of the Word to "doers" of the word. Nourished by his very body and blood, Jesus urges us to "do this in remembrance of me" (Luke 22:19).

These ten keys of discipleship are not to be understood as linear progressions but may happen concurrently and at different intensities in accord with the Holy Spirit. Conversion often happens when we least expect it.

Now that we have some foundational principles outlined, let's dive into the components of the disciple-making process, beginning by putting first things first.

How Jesus Formed Disciples

The life of Jesus constitutes a framework for the disciple-making process. What does Jesus do before inviting people to become his disciples? He goes away to pray and to discern, in conversation with his Father, whom to choose. Throughout the Gospels, Jesus regularly retreats from the world to spend time alone in prayer. He prays with the disciples, for the disciples, and over the disciples. Prayer is at the heart of the disciple-making process and our first step in the process of discipleship.

We run the risk of spending our days talking about God but not talking to God. Jesus' example shows us that taking every discipleship decision to the Father is our best and first step. We will focus in the next chapter on how to cultivate a culture of prayer, particularly intercessory prayer, in our lives, but suffice it to say, spending serious time in prayer is not an option but a necessity. Prayer keeps us grounded in our relationships with God and with one another so that we can answer Jesus' ongoing call.

A friend once said to me, "The devil calls you by your sins, but Jesus calls you by your name." Satan, as the father of lies, calls people by their shame and their mistakes, but Jesus calls each one of us with our holy potential in mind. In the Scriptures, disciples are called, not for what they did in the past but for their openness, their willingness to be coached, their faithfulness, and their potential impact. The persecutor and oppressor become pope and martyr, the tax collector becomes a Gospel writer, and simple fishermen become the greatest missionaries and evangelists the world has ever known. The Pharisees are clearly puzzled by this and say to the disciples, "Why does your teacher eat with tax collectors and sinners?" (Matthew 9:11) But when Jesus hears this, he says, "Those who are well have no need of a physician, but those who are sick. Go and learn what this means, 'I desire mercy, not sacrifice.' For I have come to call not the righteous but sinners" (Matthew 9:12–13). In the same way, each of us is called, not because of what we did in the past but for how we open ourselves to God's purposes.

Once Jesus had chosen his disciples, his first words to them were "come and see" (John 1:39). Together, they grew in friendship. It was only after the disciples had spent time with Jesus that he invited them to "follow me" (Matthew 9:9). They had to spend time with Jesus before they knew whom they were following and why. After sharing his life with them and journeying with them for three years, Jesus asked the disciples to "abide in me as I abide in you" (John 15:4) through his very body and blood in the Eucharist. It was only when the disciples had grown in spiritual maturity, through struggle and joy, that they were sent out two by two to "go and make disciples of all nations, baptizing them in the name of the Father, and of the Son and of the Holy Spirit, and teaching them to obey everything I have commanded you" (Matthew 28:19–20).

Pope Francis continues to emphasize the themes of encounter, accompaniment, and mission, all of which take place within a specific community: the parish. These words have their foundation in the process Jesus used to form disciples, which is outlined in the Scriptures. When the missionary discipleship process—using Pope Francis's terminology—and the example of Jesus are united, the framework looks like this.

Scripture	Pope Francis's Term
• "Come and see."	• Encounter
• "Follow me."	• Accompaniment
• "Remain united with me."	• Community
• "Go and make disciples."	• Mission

These stages are outlined in the document *Living as Missionary Disciples,* published in 2017 by the USCCB Committee on Evangelization and Catechesis. This is the committee on which I have served as a consultant for the past eight years. This document situates the missionary discipleship process within the person of Jesus Christ and discusses how we grow as a community of faith. When we look at Jesus' life, we can learn not only from his principles of discipleship but also the general sequence, or order, of how he formed disciples. Let's take a closer look.

What Methods Did Jesus Use to Form Disciples?

Jesus invested deeply in a small group of disciples and encouraged his disciples to do the same (see Matthew 28:18–19 and 2 Timothy 2:2). While he did speak to large crowds, most of his time was spent with the twelve disciples and with a core group within the twelve—Peter, James, and John—in whom he invested even more deeply. One by one they were called by Jesus, and two by two they were sent out to make disciples of all nations. Here is a general sequence by which Jesus formed disciples.

1. **Prayer.** Jesus prayed about whom he would choose to be his disciples. He prayed with them, for them, and over them.

2. **Call.** Jesus called the disciples, each by name and by the deepest desires of his heart. Looking upon them with love, he invited them to "come and see" him.

3. **Healing.** Jesus healed the wounds of the people by speaking to their needs and to the brokenness in their lives. He offered compassion where there had been judgment, mercy where there had been retribution, and hope when all had seemed hopeless.

4. **Proclamation.** Jesus proclaimed the Good News in word and deed. He told people about his Father and the kingdom of heaven.

5. **Friendship.** Jesus spent ample time with his disciples, eating with them, fishing with them, and getting to know them.

6. **Charisms (spiritual gifts).** Jesus helped the disciples understand their gifts, their talents, and their supernatural gifts, called charisms.

7. **Witness.** Jesus showed the disciples what to do (healing, proclaiming, teaching) by modeling experiences, values, and behaviors that the disciples could emulate.

8. **Teaching.** Jesus taught them in word and deed.

9. **Formation.** Jesus equipped them for mission (to do what he did). He encouraged them to do what he did and then to do these things continually in his name.

10. **Ongoing presence.** Jesus promised to remain united in prayer and worship with the disciples through his real presence in the Eucharist, the sacraments, and his body the Church.

Within the discipleship process are various phases of discipleship: from a beginning disciple to a growing disciple and, finally, to a more mature disciple who makes disciples of others. We are called upon to act not simply as disciples but as missionary disciples in the world. Is there a difference? Yes. Some differences are subtle, and some are more substantial. So, let's take a closer look at what we call a missionary disciple.

What Is a Missionary Disciple?

Pope Francis introduced the term "missionary disciple" in his document *Evangelii Gaudium* as follows:

> Every Christian is a missionary to the extent that he or she has encountered the love of God in Christ Jesus: We no longer say that we are "disciples" and "missionaries" but rather that we are always "missionary disciples." (#120)

In the world of social media, where your influence is often defined by how many followers you have, Jesus doesn't want to leave us where we are as followers but to form us as missionary disciples and missionary leaders who go out to share him with others. With Mass attendance rates hovering at around 30 percent or lower in many dioceses, it is clear that the majority of Catholics are not practicing the most basic and outward expressions of our faith. Missionary disciples are distinguished by their desire to go out and encounter others and make disciples and disciple-makers of others. They exercise leadership for the kingdom modeled on the life of Jesus.

This dynamic of following and leading is a lifelong process. In order to follow Jesus, we need to be attentive and watch for his cues. When we are open and willing, the Holy Spirit fills our hearts and sends us out as missionary disciples who make disciples of others. Where he leads, we follow. When we follow him, he is going to ask us to lead for him at a certain point. When he leads us, we start to become leaders of others. This call, or sending, is part of the discipleship process in which there is movement from being a disciple to being sent as a missionary disciple.

A missionary disciple emphasizes the importance of following and sharing Jesus with others. A missionary disciple inspires, equips, and forms others to be disciples and disciple-makers. Missionary disciples go beyond duty and obligation to become active missionaries of their family, friends, neighbors, and those in their wider communities. Missionary disciples are passionate in bringing Jesus to others because they love him and love the Jesus they see in other people.

Mission is not something we do; mission is at the heart of how we bring Jesus to others. It is possible for us to grow from being a disciple to a missionary disciple through the regular practice of the faith or what is known in Green Bay, Wisconsin, where I minister, as "the habits of discipleship."

Bishop David Ricken, twelfth bishop of the Diocese of Green Bay, articulated a vision for missionary discipleship entitled "Disciples on the Way" in 2014 and has been leading his diocese more deeply into a missionary paradigm through subsequent years. The Diocese of Green Bay differentiates between a disciple and a missionary disciple through ten discipleship habits.

Ten Habits of Discipleship	Disciple	Missionary Disciple
Relationship	Has a personal relationship with Jesus Christ	Introduces others to their best friend, Jesus Christ
Prayer	Makes time for prayer every day	Helps others pray
Commitment	Has a commitment to Jesus, the Church, and the Kingdom	Guides others to make a commitment to Jesus, the Church, and the Kingdom
Worship	Attends Mass at least once a week and more frequently	Invites and welcomes other to Mass and to the sacramental life of the Church
Study	Cultivates the habit of continual learning, particularly of the Scriptures and other spiritual writings	Introduces others to the great treasury of spiritual writings of the Church, especially the Scriptures
Openness	Is open and responsive to where the Holy Spirit is leading him or her and others	Helps others become more open to the Holy Spirit
Participates	Joyfully participates in the sacramental and communal life of the Church	Walks with others intentionally in faith and helps them discern where the Lord is calling them to participate
Shares	Shares personal gifts, time, and treasure with the Lord, his Church, and others	Helps others in word and deed to be generous stewards of the gifts given to us
Evangelizes	As a leader, evangelizes the world through Word, witness, works of mercy, and compassion	Provides inspiration, support, and formation for others in how to share the Good News
Serves	Serves others in the name of Jesus Christ	Guides others in the name of Jesus Christ

There is some overlap between the stages, and that is OK. No one progresses the same way and at the same pace. The disciple moves from contemplation of the divine to a sense of personal transformation to the transformation of others for the world. Clearly, these habits go beyond obligation and duty if done out of sincere love. This motivation to do and act from a position of love urges us out of ourselves for the sake of mission. But what exactly is mission?

Mission is about knowing Jesus and making him known, about loving Jesus and making his love known. Mission is about making what seems impossible possible.

Mission Not Impossible

The word *mission* comes from the Latin word *mission*, meaning "act of sending," or *mittere*, meaning "to send." From the sixteenth century, these terms became most closely associated with the Jesuits, who sent their missionaries abroad to share the gospel. Mission is intrinsic to the process of missionary discipleship because the Church herself is a community of missionary disciples; "The Church which 'goes forth' is a community of missionary disciples who take the first step, who are involved and supportive, who bear fruit and rejoice" (*Evangelii Gaudium*, #24).

One of the biggest revelations about the disciple-making process is that too often we see ourselves as a people without a mission. Missionary disciples cannot help but share their faith with others. They do not see themselves as having a mission but understand that they themselves are the mission. In one of my evangelization seminars, I ask the students to reflect on what it means to be a missionary disciple, and I challenge them to reflect on how they are a mission, not simply have a mission or are part of one. My friend Mary, who is a very dedicated director of religious education, found this exercise life-changing.

I realized that my mission was not just to do religious education. My mission is to make sure that each person knows how much God the Father loves them personally and uniquely. And I can do this anywhere! My job at the parish is religious education, but my personal mission happens where I go.

This simple but meaningful exercise is transformative because it helps ground our own vocation and call to holiness in a real way to be at the service of others. That is not an impossible mission. As Pope Francis reminds us, mission is "at once a passion for Jesus and a passion for his people" (*Evangelii Gaudium*, #268). If we live as a mission-driven people fueled by love for Jesus and for others, we can transform the world. Now, let's make that mission possible, starting with our parish community.

_ _ _ _ _ _ _ _ _ _ _ _ **TAKING ACTION** _ _ _ _ _ _ _ _ _ _ _

Pray as You Go (and Make Disciples)

Prayer to the Blessed Virgin Mary, First and Best Disciple

Mary, Star of the new evangelization, help us to bear radiant witness to communion, service, ardent and generous faith, justice and love of the poor, that the joy of the gospel may reach to the ends of the earth, illuminating even the fringes of our world. Mother of the living Gospel, wellspring of happiness for God's little ones, pray for us. Amen. Alleluia!

—adapted from *Evangelii Gaudium*, #287–288

Personal Principle

Review the ten D keys of discipleship, reflecting on each. *You can use the chapter 3 online printable resource, "The 10 Ds of Discipleship," to enhance your reflection.* www.loyolapress.com/startwithjesus Jot down your thoughts on how you can grow in your faith by exploring each key and how it relates to your life.

As an additional exercise, consider the following quote:

Mission is never the fruit of a perfectly planned program or a well-organized manual. Mission is always the fruit of a life which knows what it is to be found and healed, encountered and forgiven. Mission is born of a constant experience of God's merciful anointing.

—Pope Francis

Complete the following sentence: "I am a mission. My mission is
_____."

Parish Priority

One of my favorite quotes from Weddell's book *Forming Intentional Disciples* is from Father Damien Ference. He writes:

> All too often those of us in positions of Church leadership assume that all folks in the pews on Sundays, all the children in our grade schools, high schools and . . . in our youth groups and all the members of our RCIA team are already disciples. Many are not. The same can be said of staffs and faculties of Catholic institutions. Our people may be very active in the programs of our parishes, schools and institutions but unfortunately, such participation does not qualify for discipleship. (55)

"The same can be said for staffs and faculties of Catholic institutions." This is a difficult statement to absorb; we often mistake those who are active, even in ministry, with being missionary disciples.

As a parish team, discuss the following questions:

- Are we, as a parish team, growing as disciples? Individually and together?

- Are we allowing our fear of perfection or perhaps our inertia to prevent us from moving more deeply into mission?

- What big changes can we make as a result of what we have read in this chapter?

- What would our office hours look like if we were serious about mission?

- How can we help those who are most connected to our parish grow in their faith?

You can use the chapter 3 online printable resource "The 10 Ds of Discipleship for a Parish Team," to enhance your reflection.

www.loyolapress.com/startwithjesus

4

The Parish That Prays Together Stays Together

Now that we have outlined some of the foundations of discipleship in our own lives, let's look at our parishes and how we can assist them to move into mission.

St. Mary Parish, a rural parish in the Midwest, was getting ready to refocus its ministries at the parish and take seriously the charge to move from maintenance into mission. They had a parish team who was on fire, had read *Evangelii Gaudium* as a team, had written a pastoral framework together, and had organized a few town hall meetings with their parishioners to gather feedback and suggestions. "All seemed in order to move into this paradigm," the chair of the pastoral council told me. There seemed to be no serious issues. Yet, after stopping and starting many times, the parish could not seem to generate any forward momentum.

A week later, I met with the parish team and, after sitting through their parish council meeting for thirty minutes, began to have a clearer picture of what was missing. It was simple and stunning in its omission.

The meeting began with an Our Father and the Hail Mary and quickly moved to the business of the meeting. It seemed that there were committees for every single stage of the discipleship process. But prayer was relegated to the first five minutes of the meeting and again at closing. See a problem with this?

Prayer was a secondary endeavor and a supplement to what was considered the main work of the parish. Later, when I sat down with the pastor and talked about the situation, he admitted that the parish council, committees, and even the parish teams spent very little time in prayer. More than that, he acknowledged that there was no serious culture of intercessory prayer in the parish.

Sound familiar?

Repeat after me: **If Eucharist is the heart of parish life, then prayer is the heartbeat. Prayer is the food and fuel of missionary activity.** Repeat again.

In the typical parish, based on the many I've been involved with, the lack of a culture of prayer is found through all ministries, including our religious education and faith formation programs. "But I don't have time to pray with my students and still get all the material covered," said Susan, a catechist, exasperated when her director of religious education, Peter, asked if prayer was interwoven into her classroom. Peter assured her that it was most important to model a life of discipleship grounded in prayer. "Why?" Susan asked. "Because, without the deep breath of prayer, our students will never believe that we have internalized our faith, that we call upon the Lord in all that we do, and that it is in and through prayer that we deepen our relationship with Christ," Peter replied.

We are tempted to make prayer an afterthought rather than the first and essential step of the discipleship process in our own lives and in our parishes. This problem isn't confined to religious education; many parish and school staff confess that they do not spend time praying together or attending Mass during the day. And yet, to the outside world, most people imagine that the parish is the one place where prayer is happening regularly. It isn't, and we must acknowledge how serious this is.

If we are honest with ourselves, prayer in our parishes is often an afterthought. As long as our parishes are places where staff do not feel comfortable praying with one another and for one another, our pews are likely to remain empty. Prayer should be front and center and permeate our homes, communities, and, indeed, the world. In *Navigating the New Evangelization*, Father Cantalamessa reminds us that "prayer is essential for Evangelization because Christian preaching is not primarily the communication of doctrine, but rather the communication of existence, of a life. The one who prays without speaking evangelizes more than the one who speaks without praying" (34). In order to raise up disciples who go on to make disciples of others, our parish culture must be one of intercessory prayer. Intercessory prayer for our parishes is essential, not optional.

I would like to point out one nuance, however. We would be mistaken to think of prayer as a simple method to employ. Rather, the *Catechism of the Catholic Church* defines prayer as a "vital and personal relationship with the living and true God" (*CCC* #2558). The fullness of prayer flows out from a living relationship between a human being and God. We do not start with our own methodologies and personal acts but instead recognize that God, as the source of life and creation, is the one who begins prayer. In sharing prayer with others, we share ourselves and the source of our own being: we share God, Jesus, and the Holy Spirit with others.

What's the best way to share prayer with others? Through cultivating a culture of intercessory prayer. This term, *intercessory prayer,* might seem unfamiliar to us, but it is at the deepest heart of who we are as Christians and happens informally in our parishes all the time.

"Share Prayer": Creating a Culture of Intercessory Prayer

Quite simply, intercessory prayer is praying on behalf of others. Intercessory prayer is not just about stating what we need but also about approaching the Lord with an expectant faith. We are reminded of this in the Scriptures: "without faith it is impossible to please God, for whoever would approach him must believe that he exists and that he rewards those who seek him" (Hebrews 11:6). Intercessory prayer is not to be reserved only for serious matters but woven into the fabric of our individual lives and our parish life.

Pope Francis has spoken many times of the value and power of intercessory prayer in the Christian life: "When evangelizers rise from prayer, their hearts are more open; freed of self-absorption, they are desirous of doing good and sharing their lives with others" (*Evangelii Gaudium*, #282).

One of the best ways we can unite with others in one faith and heart is through what I call "share prayer." Like many of us, I am often asked to pray for people. For many years, I would assure the person that I would pray for him or her and would do so at night or in the morning. Many times, I had so many requests for prayer that I forgot the intentions and prayed for all those whom I had forgotten but whose names and intentions are known intimately by God. But one day I had an insight: why was I waiting to pray later when I could pray immediately instead? Rather than assuring my friends and family that I would pray for them later, I began to ask a bold but simple question: "Can we pray together now?" In all the years I have been asked to pray for someone and invited him or her to pray with me right at that moment, I have never heard a "no." The first couple of times I did this, it was incredibly uncomfortable to pray aloud with someone, but through the years I have found this to be one of the most transformative practices in strengthening my faith.

This approach has stood the test of time. My friend who is director of a Newman Center has used it for years to great effect with young adults.

How to "Share Prayer"

Picture the scenario: As you are out and about at the grocery store, you run into a friend you haven't seen in some time. As the conversation progresses, you notice that your friend seems worried and anxious. You remark on this, and the friend opens up to you and asks for your prayers. The typical response at this point is "Of course I will pray for you," and then both of you move on with the rest of your day. Uplifting someone spontaneously in prayer is not something that Catholics have been taught to do, and yet it is a part of our deepest identity as Catholics. Even for those of us in ministry, we know that we want to do something, but we don't know what to do in that moment. This isn't a particularly Catholic problem but is part of the "culture of silence" in which we do not talk with others about our faith.

The value of intercessory prayer is that it connects us more deeply to the suffering of the other person while at the same time encouraging the Lord to take hold of our lives and our situations. It can feel jarring to verbalize our innermost prayers with another person, intensifying feelings of vulnerability or inadequacy about the language we use. But it's so powerful! If we cannot share who we are in prayer, we cannot share the gospel.

Instead of relegating prayer to the future, when asked to pray for an intention, ask, "Would it be OK if I pray with you?" If they say no, move on. If they say yes, you may follow this template or improvise as the Holy Spirit moves you.

- You can call on God in the following ways: God, Lord, Father, Jesus, Holy Spirit, Heavenly, Loving, etc.

- Thank God for the person you are praying with and ask for God's blessing on him or her: "Thank you for my friend, your son/daughter of Christ. Please bless him/her and uplift him/her at this time."
- Then ask God for what the person needs, for example: "We ask you to help Ann's family make the right decisions about the nursing home" or "We ask you to help Jason, who is struggling with debt at this time."
- Express gratitude for all that God is doing: "Thank you, Lord Jesus, for revealing yourself to us" or "Thank you for your blessings on this family."
- Finish the prayer with a doxology: "We ask this through Christ our Lord" or "We ask this in Jesus' name" or "Through Our Lord Jesus Christ, your Son, who lives and reigns with the Holy Spirit, one God forever and ever" or finish with a Glory Be to the Father.

Intercessory prayer is life-changing. It is not just preparation for mission but an act of living out the gospel. Teaching friends and family to intercede for one another begins when we model and witness to one another every day. This is an easy approach that can also be taught to children effectively. So, the next time someone asks for your prayers, how about sharing a prayer with him or her instead? Praying for and with people can move mountains.

The Power of Prayer: Moving Mountains

Father Kevin, pastor of a large urban parish, called one day to talk about the parish administrative assistant: "She is really good at all the tasks assigned to her," he said, "but she can be very blunt, curt, and sometimes rude over the phone and in person." This attitude was felt not only by the parish staff but also by the parishioners. For many of us, this is a familiar situation in our parishes. We all seem to have "that one person" on our parish teams who can be difficult to work with.

Father Kevin and I talked about a couple of different options, including giving a "warning" to the individual, putting a note in her personnel file, and pursuing matters with human resources. But the more we talked, the more we realized that these solutions didn't feel right to either of us. We decided to try something different, agreeing that if the situation didn't change within two weeks, we could go to the other options.

Two weeks later, Father Kevin called me back. Not only was his administrative assistant much improved, but the disposition of other staff members had also changed. What had Father Kevin done to change matters? He had seriously and intentionally put the first step of the process of discipleship (prayer) into action. Father Kevin did three things.

- He prayed for each staff member by name, offered Mass for their intentions, and let them know that he was doing this for them.

- He made an effort to stop by each staff member's office for conversation and prayer, encouraging them to pray with one another and to share their concerns.

- He gave each staff member a special prayer that we had written together, entitled "A Prayer for Those Who Answer the Phone."

Rather than single out any particular staff member, Father Kevin had gathered his team and shared with them his hope that the parish office would truly become a place of prayer for their parishioners and for the staff. He shared that it was difficult for him to hear that his parish offices were not truly places of prayer but instead so focused on business that the needs of parishioners were not considered as they should be. He asked every single staff member to place the prayer by his or her phone and to pray it together in the morning but also individually throughout the day. This "A Prayer for Those Who Answer the Phone" goes as follows:

> Heavenly Father,
> Today there will be many people who will call our parish
>   looking for help, support, guidance, and love.
> Give me your words, Lord, so that I might be your voice to
>   those who need to hear your voice today.
> Direct my thoughts and guide my actions so that I may be
>   your hands, feet, and voice to all those who need
>   you today.
> As I answer the phone, I ask the Holy Spirit to give me the
>   words to be Christ.
> During this conversation, help me to remember how Your Son
>   welcomed the poor, the lonely, the stranger, the outcast,
>   and the difficult.
> After my conversations, Lord, I give thanks to you for helping
>   me through the day.
> Fill me with the Holy Spirit and the desire to do your will.
> We ask this in Jesus' name. Amen.

Discipleship is for every person. Those who answer the phone are the front lines of our ministries. They are the face of the parish in many ways and must be people of prayer. Those who have been away from the Catholic Church for some time will not ordinarily walk into a parish office but instead may make a phone call to talk to the parish administrative assistant or receptionist. Because of the importance of this role, it is essential that we pause during our day to recognize that we are Christ to the stranger, the poor, the lonely, the outcast, and the difficult. Taking a few moments to pray before we answer the phone helps us ground ourselves in the words of Christ: "I was hungry and you gave me food, I was thirsty and you gave me something to drink, I was a stranger and you welcomed me" (Matthew 25:35).

It is hard to pinpoint exactly what strategy was most effective in Father Kevin's parish, but his story reminds us of the importance of cultivating an atmosphere of prayer in our homes and parishes. We must intentionally welcome Christ into our workday; in doing so, we are more prepared to welcome and walk with others. Had Father Kevin called in his administrative assistant and given her a warning, it is certain that one of two things would have happened: the situation would have improved or it would not have improved. By approaching the problem first with prayer, Father Kevin found that he did not have to undertake any further course of action. Prayer had moved this mountain for him and, as a result, everyone in the office was working together more closely and was more considerate of others. Thanks be to God.

Calling 911

In all my years of ministry, I've observed that the people and the teams who regularly spend the most time in prayer are the healthiest and the most fruitful. By prayer, I mean that they employ lots of different prayer strategies to build them up, including fasting. (Fasting is what I refer to as praying with your body.) Here are some of the prayer practices that I have observed that strengthen us.

- attending Mass
- setting aside a few moments of quiet to pray at various intervals of the day (the Angelus at noon, Divine Mercy at three o'clock, the Rosary)
- taking the time to pray at a holy hour or a "holy fifteen minutes" as it works with our schedule
- fasting for one another and for the intentions of the parish
- meditating, performing *lectio divina,* intercessory prayer, praying the Liturgy of the Hours

I want to share one further strategy with you that might be helpful. I call it the 911 prayer.

By now, you might have realized that the work of making disciples is arduous, joy-filled, and, yes, exhausting. When we interact and connect with people all day such as in colleges, healthcare, or customer service, we can feel overwhelmed by the pain that we hear about. One of my campus ministers confided that the weight of the struggles of the young people he walks with feels crushing to him at times. "Sometimes I can hardly breathe," he told me. We discussed the challenges of how to let one another know that we were walking through some difficult situations, especially when those situations required that we preserve confidentiality. We settled on the 911 prayer.

The prayer is simple. When someone feels in need of prayer, they send out a group email or message with "911 Prayer" in the subject line. Once I receive that email, I pray Psalm 91 for that one person. One prayer (Psalm 91), one person (1) becomes 911.

For the days following the prayer request, I often set an alarm on my phone to pray at 9:11 a.m. and again at 9:11 p.m. Sometimes, at the invitation of the person requesting prayer, we come together to talk about what is happening. But many times we do not. Among my favorite lines from Psalm 91 are verses 14–15.

> "Because he loves me," says the Lord,
> "I will rescue him;
> I will protect him, for he acknowledges my name.
> He will call on me, and I will answer him;
> I will be with him in trouble,
> I will deliver him and honor him."

These lines have carried me through some stormy waters. It is a good reminder that if we do not nourish our relationship with a living God through prayer, our discipleship efforts will fall flat.

In the year 2000, Cardinal Joseph Ratzinger, then prefect for the Congregation for the Doctrine of the Faith, quoting Don Didimo (a parish priest), made this statement:

> Jesus preached by day, by night He prayed. . . . Jesus had to acquire the disciples from God. We ourselves cannot gather men. We must acquire them by God for God. All methods are empty without the foundation of prayer.

This principle remains true. Every great missionary enterprise that has ever taken place in the Church has been rooted in prayer. There's a lot of wisdom in the saying that we should "pray as if everything depends on God, work as if everything depends on you." It's been attributed to St. Ignatius, but regardless of whether St. Ignatius truly said this or not, it is a necessity in cultivating a culture of missionary discipleship at your parish. As the agent of evangelization, the Holy Spirit will guide our steps if we are listening in prayer. From prayer, we arise to take our next steps, having leaned into the guidance and wisdom of the Holy Spirit.

So, pray as you go and set the world on fire!

———————— TAKING ACTION ————————

Pray as You Go (and Make Disciples)

An Act of Faith, Hope, and Love

> Jesus, I believe in you.
> Jesus, I hope in you.
> Jesus, I love you.

—from the Loyola Press website

Personal Principle

For each disciple, it is essential to spend time with the Master, to listen to his words, and to learn from him always. Unless we listen, all our words will be nothing but useless chatter.

—Gaudete and Exsultate, #150

Set aside time every day to pray, blocking the time off your schedule if necessary. Work through some of the suggestions in the printable resource to help you become more prayerful. *You can use the chapter 4 online printable resource, "Prayer: Our Daily Bread," to structure your reflection.* www.loyolapress.com/startwithjesus

Parish Priority

Challenge your parish committees and organizations to pray more deeply as an intentional act of discipleship. Make prayer a nonnegotiable part of your disciple-making efforts. Shift your committees from the mere transference of information to a true communion in which all are called to holiness. Use "The Daily Disciple" printable resource as a guide.

Begin and end meetings with prayer—not a rote prayer, but intercessory prayer. Model for your parish committee what intercessory prayer looks like. Incorporate some of the strategies from this chapter, including Share Prayer and the 911 Prayer.

Don't let parish business overtake the main tasks of gathering your committees. Every sixth meeting of your parish committees should be a time for reflection and spiritual growth rather than business. At least twice yearly, prescribe a night on which members of all committees come together to pray or to hear a witness story or an inspiring talk. *You can use the chapter 4 online printable resource, "Prayer: Our Daily Bread," to structure your reflection.*

www.loyolapress.com/startwithjesus

5

Hope, Healing, and Hospitality: The Hinge Points of Discipleship

Holy Family Parish is a small rural parish located in Missouri that had steadily been declining for years, both in age and in energy. When Father Dave was assigned there in the middle of the year due to a "priest personnel issue," many parishioners remarked that it was "the final nail in the coffin" of Holy Family. Over a six-year period, a series of priests had moved in and out of the parish. The parishioners' spirits were at a low ebb. Father Dave knew that he had the challenge of Sisyphus ahead of him but was determined to make a difference. One year later, I paid this beautiful but remote parish a visit in preparation for a parish mission that they had asked me to lead. To my surprise, I found not a parish in the grip of rigor mortis but a vibrant, welcoming, and warm community that was growing. Not only was the office a bustling place with various parishioners coming and going, but Mass and confession attendance had increased and the numbers of those joining the parish were steadily improving. Some parishioners who had drifted away were coming back to Mass, and many remarked that, rather than death, a "parish resurrection" had occurred. It seemed to be a miracle, but it was nothing of the sort. It was a true case of the ordinary becoming extraordinary!

Sitting with Father Dave over a cup of tea, I asked him to share with me what had happened at the parish. Expecting a tale of perhaps a financial windfall coupled with a strategic vision and increased resources, instead I learned from Father Dave that three emphases had led to their success. "Many parishioners had become demoralized," he said.

> This is a place that has always had strong communal bonds where everyone knows everyone, but we were slipping. Instead of focusing on programs, we emphasized relationships and three very specific things: hope, healing, and hospitality. These three things became the basis of renewal.

Among the most effective strategies to reach people are invitation, welcoming, and relationship building. Father Dave had chosen to focus on three distinct issues.

- **Hope:** to connect, uplift, and inspire his parish staff and parishioners
- **Healing:** to bring relief to all those struggling with restlessness, busyness, suffering, addiction, sadness, and fear
- **Hospitality:** to meet people where they are and embrace them as brothers and sister in Christ

The open and welcoming sanctuary that the parish wanted to become needed what I call hinge points to open the door for change. One Sunday, Father Dave looked out at the sea of faces and realized how tired many people were. Coming to Mass on Sunday was one of the few times that these families spent in prayer together. Rather than chide them for not being more active parishioners, he offered hope, healing, and hospitality as a way to encourage, uplift, and nourish. He was also familiar with the stages of discipleship and knew that these specific methodologies were especially important for those in what is called pre-evangelization. Pre-evangelization refers to the work we do to make evangelization possible; it's work that helps people become aware of Jesus' desire to have a relationship with each person.

In chapter 9, we will look at pre-evangelization in more detail, but for now, let's look at each hinge point.

Hope Springs Eternal

Sitting in the airport waiting for a flight one day, I took out my book and began to read. After a few minutes, the gentleman sitting beside me leaned over and said, "Excuse me, I couldn't help but notice from the cover of your book that you might be a Christian." Somewhat startled by his observation, I replied, "Yes, I am a Christian; in fact, I am a Catholic."

"Can I ask you a question?" the man asked.

"Go ahead." I tucked away my book, ready to listen.

"Do you feel hopeful?" he asked. I was surprised at the question. But I took a deep breath and said that, while I have up and down days like everyone else, for the most part I am filled with hope because of my faith.

As I looked into his face, I sensed that he was struggling with something and so I asked, "Do you believe in God?"

"I'm not sure. Sometimes I think that I do, but lately I have not felt his presence in my life. I feel that I have nothing to hope for."

"Hope has a name," I said.

"What is it?"

"Jesus."

We spent the next fifty minutes talking. He shared with me the pain of a broken marriage and a job that leaves him feeling empty most of the time. Although raised Catholic, he had not been to church in many years. Before he left to make his connection, I promised that I would pray for him and keep in touch. Recently, he told me that he has started to return to Mass. The overwhelming sense of peace he feels when he is there gives him the strength to keep going.

It is difficult to be a Christian in a postmodern, relativistic world in which those who identify as religious are marginalized or written off as being out of touch or old-fashioned. In our secular world, suspicion and mistrust of Christianity, and especially of Catholicism, have become much more common, particularly in the wake of the clergy sex abuse scandals and their cover-up. The postmodern journey of conversion usually begins when there is a bridge of trust with another Christian, a positive connection to a community of faith or something identifiably Christian. This often takes place outside of church—in a group setting or in commonplace activities such as at the gym or the coffee shop. I find that when I travel and have some spiritual reading out, others often engage me in conversation about their lives. Most often, I simply listen, but I also share how God has worked in my life and, when appropriate, I pray with the person.

Hope is not wishful thinking but a certainty that comes with living our faith day by day. Hope is a virtue, a gift God gives us that grows out of faith and manifests itself in love for others. Living in hope means that we can give a name to our hope: Jesus Christ, who offers us comfort and strength. Each of us can become a source of hope for others.

Hope in a Well

On a regular basis, we encounter those in a state of "pretrust" who may be passively participating in activities or engaging marginally with Christians but have not yet built bonds of trust with Christians or the Church. Keeping a warm and inviting presence with those in the pretrust stage is critical, or they will not move closer to God. Trust is the foundation of all relationships, and discipleship happens only at the speed of trust. Debating religion with someone who is in this delicate stage can be harmful. While we may win an argument, we may well lose the person. When we close our hearts to people and treat them with contempt, neglect, or indifference, it reinforces their perception that we—and thus, the Church—are not deserving of trust.

We see how Jesus builds a bond of trust with the Samaritan woman. He approaches her in the heat of the day (according to John 4:6), and she develops an initial trust in the man who dares to speak to her, a Samaritan and a woman, clearly a person outside the circle of a Jewish male's acceptable companions.

The Samaritan woman becomes more open to the possibility of change when Jesus indicates that he knows all about her situation yet does not appear to condemn her outright. (Otherwise, why would he even speak to her?) There is something about Jesus that draws her in. Not only does Jesus quench her thirst for water but he quenches her thirst for "living water." He gives her hope and does not shame her. She wants to know more, and she wants to tell others all about the man she has met and what she has experienced in that conversation at the well. She runs to share the Good News that she is loved, that we are all loved by Jesus. Her compelling testimony is now offered to those who have not met Jesus and yet can still encounter him in and through the woman's story.

What do you see when you look into a well? If you peer down into the inky blackness, all you see is darkness. But if you are at the bottom of the well, what do you see? Light. A sliver of light is visible when you look up from the blackness. Jesus and the Samaritan woman met at a place where light and darkness came together. In each of us, light and darkness also come together in our desire to live out the Christian life and to avoid sin. Jesus was clearly able to see into the heart of the Samaritan woman and encourage her to look up and see the light. When we encounter others, rather than look down into the well of their darkness and sin, we can encourage them to look up and see the light. This is what it means to be a bridge of hope and a light for others.

What does a parish centered on the virtue of hope look like? This is a difficult question to answer, but Father Dave says that praying with an expectant faith and with hope is the first step. Dismayed in his first couple of weeks at the parish, he looked out at the empty pews and began to pray for them to be filled with new and returning parishioners. Each day, this tenacious pastor walked up and down the rows in his Church "praying the pews." He asked his parish staff to do the same and join him. He then shared this approach with his parishioners and asked them to "spiritually adopt" the pew that they regularly sat in and pray for those who would sit in their pew. His parishioners took this a step further and regularly asked, "Who's new to the pew?" and reached out to welcome those they didn't know. In addition, Father Dave offered the following:

- prayer services for those who struggle with or have family members or friends struggling with addiction, mental illness, serious illness, and abuse
- simple homilies that uplifted, encouraged, challenged, and supported his parishioners by focusing on day-to-day experiences
- encouragement for parish staff members to be at school and community functions such as sporting events, concerts, recitals, and graduation ceremonies
- visibility at local restaurants and coffee shops to spend time with people
- intercessory petitions for each Mass that spoke to real needs in the local community

Despite all that the world faces, Pope St. John Paul II reminds us, "Humanity is able to hope. Indeed, it must hope: the living and personal Gospel, Jesus Christ himself, is the good news and the bearer of joy that the Church announces each day" (*Christifideles Laici*, 7).

We and our parishes must be places where all people are plunged into the merciful love of Jesus, which brings hope. This is what Father Dave and his parish did so faithfully and simply.

Healing: Try a Little Tenderness

A loud knock on our front door woke my husband and me from sleep. On our front doorstep was our friend Lucy, who was crying. "I found Daniel cheating with another woman," she said. Daniel was Lucy's husband of nineteen years. Over the next few days, Lucy and I had some in-depth conversations about the direction of her life. As we talked about her life and faith, she said that she wished she could be happy in her marriage.

"You and Wayne are a great team," she said to me. "I see how you relate to each other, and I want that realness. What's the secret?"

"He, she, and Thee, all things in three," I said. "It's an old Irish proverb that basically means that in every marriage there are three persons: husband, wife, and God. God is the center of our marriage, and it's our faith in God and in each other that pulls us through." Faith is what has held my husband and me together through the death of a child, our daughter's chronic illness, and the death of beloved family members.

During this conversation, I invited Lucy to come with our family to church if she was interested. "But I don't want to go to a class at the parish or go to Mass," she said. "I haven't been in years."

"How about sitting in a quiet place and telling Jesus what's on your heart?" I asked. And so that afternoon, I found myself sitting silently by my friend as she poured out her heart in an empty church in front of the Blessed Sacrament. The only thing I said to her was, "Give Jesus the one burden in your heart that you want to be free of." She nodded. From that moment, Lucy began to find her way back to the Church, beginning with sitting in silence in front of Jesus, the Divine Healer.

Lucy's story reveals a couple of important points for us. While her story is still being written, healing is instrumental in the conversion process. Not ready for Mass or a small faith-sharing study, Lucy found that silence, time, and the power of the Blessed Sacrament made all the difference. So, too, did friends who were willing to walk with her on her journey and encourage her along the way.

Reaching out to those who are broken is another way we reach out to those on the margins. In the Gospels, we read that Jesus constantly spent time healing the blind, the lame, the paralyzed, the hard-hearted, the angry, and the despairing. He never turned away anyone who needed healing, and neither should we. Our parishes should be places of healing love and mercy. During a Mass at Casa Santa Marta on February 5, 2015, Pope Francis described the Church as a "field hospital" that requires, he said, "healing the wounded hearts, opening doors, freeing [people], and saying that God is good, forgives all, is our Father, is tender, and is always waiting for us." The first thing Jesus did after the Resurrection was to reveal his wounds to the disciples. As a Church, we must reclaim this healing dimension in our parishes so that we can warm the hearts of those who have been wounded.

The Parish as a Sanctuary of Healing

We and our parishes can meet people's need for sanctuaries of healing and mercy. Christians who walk with people through divorce, remarriage, grief, and all forms of suffering will find themselves growing and helping others grow into disciples of Jesus. As leaders, we should not be afraid of entering "the tomb" of suffering of another person and reconciling this suffering to the Cross so that we experience the Resurrection. We can, in our very person, be a balm for those who are tired, weary, and struggling.

We can become a fountain of healing for others by offering encouragement and praying with them when the time is right. Also, we need to use our words carefully. Words are like splinters: once spoken they can wound deeply and painfully, so we should be especially careful when tempted to be judgmental. We are often tempted to write off people who are not living according to our high standards. When we're in judgmental mode, we are likely to treat people rudely. St. Ambrose reminds us that "no one heals himself by wounding another"; other wise teachers point out that pain that is not transformed through patience, prayer, and consideration for others is often transferred. Like a splinter lodged in our hand, a small utterance of scorn or condemnation can wound a person and stay in his or her memory for a long time. We are called to exercise good judgment and hold ourselves and others in our faith community to a higher standard, but God alone is the judge of others' lives. Building relationships takes time, and you may need to prudently hold off certain conversations until the person is ready.

Jesus is the Divine Physician and ultimate healer; we are healed by his own wounds (1 Peter 2:24). Making sure that the parish includes opportunities for healing services and easy access to the sacrament of reconciliation is tremendously important in reaching our parishioners and nonparishioners. So too are "healing services" where the Blessed Sacrament is exposed and people are able to voice or record (such as in a journal) matters that are weighing on their hearts.

Father Dave's parish is a great illustration of the power of attraction coupled with credible, hopeful witness. The Church grows by the energy of Christ's love, not by the power of ideologies, as Pope Emeritus Benedict XVI remarked during the inauguration of the Fifth General Conference of Latin American Bishops at the Marian shrine of Aparecida, Brazil, on May 13, 2007. "Leading with the 'yes' of who we are," says Father Dave, "is always more powerful than telling people what we say 'no' to."

Our yes can be the welcome mat to the people waiting to take the next step in their faith journey.

Hospitality: First Impressions Matter

A popular expression is "First impressions are lasting impressions." This is true of parish hospitality. Unfortunately, hospitality has become synonymous with coffee and donuts after Mass or relegated to a committee such as the stewardship committee or the hospitality committee. Not only has this mindset absolved us of the need to go out of our comfort zone to welcome others, but it also reinforces the mindset that hospitality is something only certain people do. Hospitality is *who we are* as the people of Christ.

A couple of years ago, I was hosting a conference at a parish church. Midway through the day, I took a break from the conference hall and sat in the narthex of the church. As I was sitting there, a woman came in and set up a small table. She explained that she was a member of the hospitality committee and that they took turns to welcome those who came into the church to view the magnificent stained-glass windows and art in the church building. Visitors signed a little guest book and were given a self-guided tour brochure to help them navigate their way around the church. Sounds welcoming, right?

After a couple of moments, the door squeaked open and a man peered around it. "I heard that this is a place that I can warm up in," he said. As he entered the narthex, it became clear that he was homeless. His hair was disheveled, and he carried a sleeping bag on his back. The odor of his suffering permeated the narthex. "This isn't a warming shelter, but if you want to go into the church to pray, you may do so," the lady said sharply. The man nodded and went into the church.

She lifted the phone. "Can you send someone over here?" she said. I presumed that she was calling the parish office. The next words out of her mouth are words I will never forget.

"There is an undesirable in the building," she said.

An undesirable. Jesus wept.

After this interchange, the pastor and the deacon from the parish came over and recognized how cold and hungry the man was. They offered him food and drink and a place to rest. They thanked him for his honesty. I left the narthex and went into the church, where I cried for some time.

This moment was a powerful lesson in what can happen when the gospel mandate for radical hospitality has been reduced to a human construct. Jesus showed up in his own house in the form of a homeless man and was not recognized. Not only did we not recognize Jesus, but his unexpected presence exposed our hard-heartedness and stinginess. Jesus also exposed my own lack of courage as a leader by waiting for the correct designated person to respond rather than responding myself.

True hospitality is not about coffee and donuts or hearts and flowers, as my friend Jane Angha, executive director of Ministry Blueprints, often reminds me. Jane says that abundant hospitality "sets the stage for an encounter with Christ." Hospitality flows from charity and is about welcoming Christ, who is deep within every person we encounter. We need to train our parishioners to be hospitable and help them see Christ in everyone and welcome all to God's house, in Jesus' name. The parish is not just our house but a home with "many dwelling-places" (John 14:2), given to all people but especially to the wounded, the difficult, the angry, the broken, and the lost.

Pope Francis reminds us that the parish is a "sanctuary where the thirsty come to drink" (*Evangelii Gaudium*, #28). Our parishes ought to be places where we can drink in the person of Christ in others, particularly those who make us a little uncomfortable. Our parishes should be places where the least of all can quench the thirst of their grief, joy, losses, sorrows, and wounds. Our parishes should become sanctuaries capable of warming hearts and bodies in love.

Pew Card Hospitality

Throughout Scripture, we find that welcoming the stranger is the true test of hospitality. Many of our parishes do a wonderful job of welcoming families to Mass on Sunday and should be commended for this. But we can always do more. At Father Dave's parish, there is a card in the pew with this message:

> To our parish families with young children,
>
> We welcome you to the celebration of the Mass, where we receive Jesus Christ in the Eucharist. The word *eucharist* means "thanksgiving," and as you celebrate with us and your children, we thank you for your presence here among us.
>
> Children are especially close to the heart of Jesus, so don't feel you have to stifle those wiggles and giggles in God's house!
>
> Children learn liturgical behavior by copying you, so quietly explain the parts of the Mass, sing the songs, and participate as best you can! Please use the card "The Meaning of the Mass" in the pew to help you. If you need to leave Mass to calm your child, feel free to do so, but please come back.
>
> Remember, the way that we welcome children in Church directly affects their faith, what they think about the Mass, and by extension Christ. Let them know that they are at home in this sacred gathering.
>
> To our parishioners—a smile and a word of encouragement is a joy to parents with small, active children. Let them know that they are welcome here.
>
> On the front of this card is a simple prayer for the family. You can pray it here after Communion or take this card with you to pray with your family at home.

This reminds us that true hospitality calls for an openness, a change of heart, a conversion. In meeting the rich young man, Jesus "looked steadily at him and loved him" (Mark 10:17–22). Jesus probably sensed that the young man was not ready to give up everything and follow him, but he still looked on him with love. Love is at the center of hospitality, healing, and hope. These qualities become the hinge points on the door of faith.

_ _ _ _ _ _ _ _ _ _ _ _ **TAKING ACTION** _ _ _ _ _ _ _ _ _ _ _

Pray as You Go (and Make Disciples)

> Jesus,
> Help me to be more hospitable.
> Help me to welcome strangers into my life, to believe in
>   blessings in disguise, to see all of life as opportunity and
>   promise.
> Help me to be you to the lost, the least, the last,
>   and—yes—even the difficult.
> Surprise me! Let me entertain angels. Better yet, may I
>   entertain you! Amen.
>
> —adapted from Sr. Melanie Svoboda, *Religion Teachers' Journal*,
>   April/May 1995

Personal Principle

Healing, hope, and hospitality are the hinge points that open the door of our hearts to the Lord and to others. It is important for us to connect these three elements so that we help others discover and follow Jesus. We clearly see this in the story of the Roman centurion who begs Jesus for healing—not for himself but for his boy servant in Matthew 8:5–11: *"Lord, I am not worthy to have you enter under my roof; but only say the word and my servant will be healed."*

You can use the chapter 5 online printable resource, "Hope, Healing, Hospitality," to enhance your reflection.
www.loyolapress.com/startwithjesus

Parish Priority

When we as a parish consider the families who have left our parish, have quit our faith formation programs, or have stopped coming to Mass, have we reflected on the true reasons they might have left? Has anyone spoken to these people? In the days ahead, pray as a parish team about making personal contact with them to ask why they left. Only undertake this action, however, if the parish team is willing to listen and make the necessary changes. This process takes courage but will be a help to all the parishioners and families entrusted to your care.

A key part of being a hope-filled and welcoming community is being able to walk with people in their daily struggles. Many parishes are open at times that are not convenient for our parishioners or potential parishioners. Consider the typical hours that your parish is open. As a parish team, reflect on hours that might better serve the needs of your parishioners or those you are hoping to attract. What changes do you need to make?

Conduct an assessment of your parish culture, particularly what is experienced at Sunday Mass. *You can use the chapter 5 online printable, "Sunday Culture Assessment" to enhance your reflection.* (www.loyolapress.com/startwithjesus) Another way to assess your parish culture is to find someone who has not visited your parish before. Encourage this person to be a "mystery shopper" by checking out the parish online through its website and social media profile and in person at Mass and by calling to get information about the parish. Have an honest conversation about this person's experience, using the information he or she collected. Identify key areas for growth and possibilities.

6

The Art of Accompaniment

The words of the song "Companions on the Journey" often come to me as I travel around the diocese visiting parishes and schools. This song was sung regularly in my parish in Ireland when I was growing up. Although I don't hear it often these days, I still think the opening lines are a beautiful testimony to accompanying others in faith: "We are companions on the journey, breaking bread and sharing life; and in the love we bear is the hope we share for we believe in the love of our God" (Carey Landry).

Knowing who we are means knowing who we are in relation to others. The French philosopher Gabriel Marcel said that the term *homo sapiens,* which is used to describe the human person, presents a diminished understanding of the human person in the modern era of serious technological and social advances. "Persons with knowledge" seems a bit of a sparse description of the human person, in all fairness! In his book *Homo Viator,* Marcel proposes that we be called *homo viator,* which means a "being on the way."

To see myself as a pilgrim goes much further than recognizing and accepting my existence; it also recognizes the givenness of my existence. We are neither the center nor the origin of our existence but rather beloved children of God. God, who brings meaning from nothingness, gifts us with presence instead of void and hope where there is despair. We are not yet where we need to be but are persons "on the way" as disciples through life. We are a pilgrim people walking the road of life together, people for others and with others traveling together on the path of life. This is what it means to "accompany others," a term Pope Francis uses frequently. In *Evangelii Gaudium* (#169), Pope Francis writes, "The Church will have to initiate everyone—priests, religious and laity—into this 'art of accompaniment' which teaches us to remove our sandals before the sacred ground of the other" (cf. Exod. 3:5).

Elements of Accompaniment

What characteristics distinguish the art of accompaniment? Any person—not only the ordained or vowed religious—can accompany others. But it's more than simply being there.

Art. Accompaniment is not an exact science but an art. It looks different to each person and progresses differently from person to person. To use a metaphor that we introduced earlier, accompaniment is not like baking a cake and following a recipe exactly. It progresses at its own pace, depending on the person you are walking with.

Awakening. We don't somehow bring God's presence to another person. We help awaken that person to the reality of God's presence. Cardinal Bergoglio, who became Pope Francis, said on August 31, 2010, that "it is always good to recall that that child, that youth and that adult that God puts on our path is not a glass that we must fill with content or a person to conquer. The Lord already dwells in their heart, given that he always precedes us." This is an important point to remember: God is with each person and walks ahead of us in every encounter whether we recognize his presence or not. Awakening others to the presence of God in their lives is a delight and a joy for us.

Empowering and equipping. To move adults toward a deeper commitment to Christ, it is important to empower and equip them with the tools to talk to other adults about their faith. Giving concrete language and strategies to engage people in discussions about faith will go a long way toward helping adults come to a mature faith. Not to mention that these discussions will help strengthen the family as parents are equipped to share their faith with their children and accompany them as part of their baptismal responsibility.

Listening. Accompaniment demands that we listen carefully to where people are in their journey and to meet them there, uniting with them in their daily concerns and walking side by side on life's path. We must listen attentively as they speak of their joy, hopes, and fears. The first step of listening is to be present, not simply quiet. Consciously attune your presence to the person you are with and ask the Lord to guide your conversation so that you can receive what you need to hear.

Openness. Accompaniment recognizes that each person brings something of himself or herself to the conversation, whether as a catechist or the one to be catechized, whether as the evangelizer or the one to be evangelized. Both learn from the other because "where two or three are gathered in my name, I am there among them" (Matthew 18:20). In *Evangelii Gaudium*, Pope Francis speaks of "attitudes which foster openness to the message: approachability, readiness for dialogue, patience, a warmth and welcome which is nonjudgmental" (#165). Openness to the other is always openness to God.

Prayer. Accompaniment relies heavily on prayer, calling on the power of the Holy Spirit and becoming comfortable with intercessory prayer. Jesus' whole life was a lesson in prayer.

Questioning. Employ the Socratic method of asking questions in your accompaniment efforts. Consider that "in the New Testament, Jesus asked 183 questions, gave 3 answers, and answered 307 questions with a question in return, like a true rabbi" (*Forming Intentional Disciples*, 147). Questions encourage natural curiosity and draw people deeper into the encounter with Christ. We find in the Scriptures that Jesus cultivates curiosity and leaves people wanting more—more wisdom, more questions to ponder, more to consider, more to behold. In short, more of him. Questions have a way of getting to the heart of the matter and helping people focus on why they believe what they believe. Pose interesting questions and listen attentively to people as they voice their hopes, fears, and dreams.

Following are examples of questions Jesus used:

- What do you want me to do for you?
- Who do you say that I am?
- Where is everyone?
- Has no one condemned you?
- What are you looking for?
- How do you read the law?
- How much do you love me?

Trust. We must trust the Holy Spirit and the power of prayer to guide us as we walk with others. Accompaniment is not just for accompaniment's sake, but rather it is always at the service of evangelization and mission. Our goal is to form disciples who go out to share their faith with others. This foundation must rest on trust so that we can build lasting relationships and embrace the hearts of those we serve.

Within the discipleship process, we must provide for accompaniment. It is highly relational and progresses at the pace set by those who are walking together. Mentoring, coaching, and working one-on-one with others or in small groups need to be part of all our discipleship efforts so that they are truly evangelizing. Jesus practiced the art of accompaniment par excellence and so should we, especially with our children and grandchildren, who ask many questions of us.

Focus on Fundamental Human Need and Desire

As we accompany others on the journey of faith, we must address basic human needs and desires when we make the case for believing in Jesus and seeking salvation within the Church. As we encounter every person, certain questions often lie in the unspoken consciousness of those who are seeking to find meaning in life, are seeking a relationship with Christ, or are curious about the teachings of the Church.

- Why does it matter if we have faith? Does faith speak to our deepest longings, hopes, and fears? Why do we exist?

- Who is Jesus Christ? What difference does it make if I believe in him? Is Jesus more than just a "good guy"? Why do I need a Savior?

- What difference will faith make in the end? What happens when we die? Can't I be a good person without believing in religion?

- How does the Catholic Church speak to major life issues? How does it help me to find meaning and understanding? How does being a part of the Catholic Church make my life better?

Many of us begin conversations about faith starting not at the top of the list, with the hunger of each person's heart, but at the bottom, with Church teaching. Take, for example, the following scenario. A friend questions the Church's teaching on sexuality and asks, "Why does the Church care about premarital sex?" Tough question, right?

Many of us immediately respond with an answer that begins with something like "The Church teaches us X, Y, and Z." From there, we often move to talking about eternal life. Rarely do we talk about what Jesus said, and rarely if ever do we connect what Jesus says to the longings of the person's heart.

However, for many, including youth and young adults who place a high premium on experiences, beginning with Church teaching does not engage hearts or earn you the right to be heard. This does not mean that there is no place for addressing questions about the Church—there is a time and a place for that. But for those who are curious about faith, it's always best to begin with the person's longings—the reason he or she is even asking a question. This approach is modeled in the *United States Catholic Catechism for Adults*. The first chapter of the USCCA is titled "My Soul Longs for You, O God," which is taken from Psalm 42:2, and subtitled "The Human Quest for God." On page 3 of the USCCA it states: "People have always asked fundamental questions" and outlines a number of helpful questions that people wrestle with: "Who am I? Where did I come from? Where am I going? Why do I need to struggle to achieve my goals? Why is it so hard to love and be loved? What is the meaning of sickness, death, and evil? What will happen after death?" We are urged to "become aware of the mysterious yearning of the human heart" (USCCA, 3).

Also, consider that in the New Testament the word *church* is mentioned more than one hundred times, while the word *Jesus* is mentioned more than nine hundred times, depending on the translation. This should tell us something of a methodology to employ in engaging people for Christ. If you reflect on conversations about your faith, what areas of Church life do you spend the most time discussing? From my experience, it is often the ecclesial questions that take up the most time. Rarely do we talk about how to engage people's real needs and how to put those needs in conversation with Jesus, especially because those needs are so varied.

An "Etsy" Approach

Etsy is an online market that focuses on handcrafted and unique one-of-a-kind items that are not found in regular stores or on Amazon.com. This shift from cookie-cutter to boutique approach is one that Jesus modeled with the disciples. Jesus invested deeply in a few people and tailored his advice and discipleship development to their unique needs. With Peter, he was direct and blunt, often challenging this hot-headed, impatient man to go beyond his comfort zone. With John, the beloved disciple, Jesus permitted him the intimacy of leaning against his breast during the Last Supper so that John could listen to the life within all life. With the disciples on the road to Emmaus, Jesus teaches us that others are most open to new insights only after they have been heard, respected, and honored.

This may mean for a time that when someone says something that is not quite correct, instead of correcting the person right away and shutting down him or her, you listen to understand, not just to respond. Is there a role for correction and fraternal charity in our accompaniment efforts? Absolutely. But remember that you can correct someone fraternally only if you *are* fraternal, meaning brotherly, with them!

As such, our approach should be less about mass-produced programs that seek to move everyone along uniformly and more of an "Etsy" or boutique approach that emphasizes the unique needs and gifts of each person, balanced by a willingness to speak to the pressing issues of the day. Jesus spoke to the relevant cultural issues of the day, whether it was to Jews, Gentiles, slaves, or free men and women. He spoke about marriage, divorce, violence, and money. He spoke about the political systems, brokenness, heartache, and apathy. When Jesus encountered difficult situations, the conversations often happened in private—such as with the woman at the well who was living with a man who was not her husband, and with Nicodemus, whom Jesus spoke with at night as a way to preserve the elder's dignity.

The disciples lived, walked, ate, drank, and slept in close quarters with Jesus for three years. Yet, we operate as if people will become disciples after going through a weekend retreat or if "they will only read this particular book." Can this happen? Sure, but it is a rarity. The same is true of our use of mass-produced programs that rely on an approach that emphasizes age rather than readiness. We imagine that if we watch a ten-week DVD series with our youth, a disciple will pop out the other side of our time together. Discipleship does not happen this way, my friends. Considering what happened with the disciple Judas Iscariot, we see that even Jesus did not have a 100 percent success rate.

As we are reminded by Pope Francis, "the pace of this accompaniment must be steady and reassuring, reflecting our closeness and our compassionate gaze which also heals, liberates and encourages growth in the Christian life" (*Evangelii Gaudium*, #169). This may mean that our formation processes move from being a mile wide and an inch deep to becoming smaller and more intimate, where more fruitful conversation can take place. This is a challenge for our religious education programs, and yet we know that when parishes move to small-group formation balanced by larger occasional gatherings, ample opportunities arise for people to develop more intimate relationships with one another. One of the best strategies we can use to accompany others and strengthen our own faith is to discover and share our story of faith.

What's the Story? What's YOUR Story?

Janet was a communications professional who had worked in an insurance corporation for many years before becoming a communications director for three large parishes. One day I asked her to share her story with me. "I don't know if I have ever thought about that before," she said. "I know it must sound odd given that I have spent twenty-three years in the world of communications and am an active Catholic, but honestly, I've never been asked this question."

"Have you ever fallen in love, had your heart broken, or lost someone you loved?" I asked. She said yes, and I reminded her that each of us has a story of faith. What followed was about two hours of conversation as Janet and I talked about her faith and her relationship with God, Jesus, the Holy Spirit, and the Catholic Church.

If a woman who has spent her entire career telling stories through branding, marketing, and interesting graphics has difficulty sharing her story of faith, it's not surprising that many of us will find it hard to do so. I am no longer surprised when Catholics who have been active in their parishes for many years tell me that they have never been asked to share their stories of faith or that they are not sure how to identify their own story. Sharing our personal story of faith seems to be incredibly difficult for Catholics, even for parish leaders. But storytelling is the oldest form of education, and, in our faith, we share the ultimate story of faith: the love story between God and his people.

Unpacking our story of faith is a necessary step for our own spiritual growth, of course, but it is also a wonderful way to evangelize and witness to our friends, family, and children. Sharing our story of faith is a gift both for the storyteller and for the listener, for it is in the sharing of our stories that communal bonds are strengthened, relationships are deepened, our faith is nourished, and God's movement in our lives is revealed. In fact, according to *Go and Make Disciples*, the USCCB's national plan on Catholic evangelization, we all are a story of faith. Telling stories is a strategy of attraction rather than promotion, drawing listeners and readers toward what fascinates their hearts. It truly brings the art of accompaniment alive.

We cannot expect our parish leaders and parishioners to share their own stories of faith and connect their stories to the Good News if they have not been taught how to do this. Likewise, we cannot expect our catechists or faith-sharing facilitators to tell effective stories from Scripture or stories of the saints and connect these stories to the events of their own lives if they have not been given these skills. True, sharing our faith with others can seem like a daunting task—but it doesn't have to be! People are often far less interested in your knowledge of the Catholic faith than they are in your experience of it. Outside of your actions, your story is the most powerful means by which you can evangelize.

In *The Catechist's Backpack: Spiritual Essentials for the Journey*, which I cowrote with Joe Paprocki, we help people share their story of faith using the following acronym:

Structure

Trial

Openness

Redemption and Renewal

You-nique

Structure. Every story needs structure. You can structure your story by highlighting the most significant experiences in your life.

- Name two or three times when you felt clearly the presence of God before, during, or after an experience.
- Think of a passage or story from Scripture that speaks to or sheds light on each experience.

Trial. Now that you have several specific experiences in mind to help structure your story of faith, focus on the aspect of trial in your story.

- How was your faith challenged in any of these experiences?
- Name two things that helped you persevere in this time of trial.

Openness. At some point during your experience, darkness turned to light and you began to be more open and accepting of your situation. Identify the turning point. What happened?

- Who or what helped you become more open to God's presence?

Redemption and Renewal. During every period of trial, there comes a time when we feel redeemed and renewed.

- Identify the moment you came to feel peace about your experience. How did this peace come?
- Which Person of the Trinity did you feel the presence of most powerfully through this experience? Why?

You-nique. Your story of faith is unique, and yet at the same time it is universal.

- What makes your story unique?
- In what sense is your unique story universal? In other words, how is it part of the larger story of salvation revealed in Scripture?
- What do you believe to be the central message of your story?
- What impact are you hoping this story will have on others?

If our goal is to form disciples who go on to become disciple-makers, we should share this passion and reverence for storytelling. The printable resource for this chapter lays out a simple process to discover and unpack your own story of faith that you can use to help others share their stories in the parish. While the events of our lives have the potential to be faith formative, many of us often engage in these events without bringing into focus our own faith or our personal relationship with Christ.

Everyone has a story to tell. If simple fishermen were able to do it, we can do likewise! God is the author of life and, in a real sense, the author of each of our stories. We are called to help write and tell this story to accompany others on their journey. Every day is an opportunity to begin anew, for each day is a page and each week is a chapter in the story of God's love for us.

_____ TAKING ACTION _____

Pray as You Go (and Make Disciples)

God our Father, Creator of story and the author of each one of our stories,

As the word became flesh and dwelt among us, guide me to see you in my story and the stories of others.

Help me to live in your Word, to listen carefully to your still, small voice, and to practice the power of pause as you speak to all people.

We ask this through the intercession of Mary, Mother of the Word, as we pray "Hail Mary . . ."

Personal Principle

Start by listening to adults and let the stories of their lives and the hungers of their hearts inspire pastoral care and inform catechetical programming. Reach out to those whom society often neglects.

*—Our Hearts Were Burning Within Us: A Pastoral Plan for
Adult Faith Formation in the United States*, #80, USCCB

Choose one person from your life who is not practicing his or her faith. Work through your story of faith and how you might share part of your story with this person.

You can use the chapter 6 online printable resource, "My Story of Faith," to enhance your reflection. www.loyolapress.com/startwithjesus

Parish Priority

As a parish team, set aside some time to work through your own stories of faith. At each staff meeting over a period of a few weeks, choose one or two people who will share part of their stories of faith until each person has had a chance to share his or her story. After the person has shared, each person on the parish team should have an opportunity to offer a word of encouragement, thanks, and prayer for the storyteller.

You can use the chapter 6 online printable resource, "Our Story of Faith," to enhance your reflection. www.loyolapress.com/startwithjesus

7

Missionary Discipleship and Culture Change

Nervously, I pushed the rusty doorbell. The door was answered with a smile by a pastor who hollered to the small group gathered inside: "It's the new evangelization lady from the diocese." I made myself as comfortable as I could in a small room with fifteen pastors already seated in it. "Julianne is here to tell us all about what we can do as disciples with the context of the new evangelization in mind," one of them said. So, as best I could, I began to communicate the urgency of being a Catholic people who start with Jesus in our lives and our parishes.

When I paused, a hand went up.

"Yes, Father Jim, please go ahead," I said.

"Julianne, I've been a pastor for twenty-seven years. During that time, someone from the diocese has come out to tell us that we need to focus on youth, then young adults, then Catholic schools, then stewardship, and now discipleship," he said. "Isn't this just the latest trend or fancy of the diocese? I can't help thinking that if we just keep our heads down and keep going the same way that we have always done, the diocese will just get bored with this new theme and move on to something else."

Talk about naming the elephant in the room! What followed was an intense and direct conversation, as you can imagine. By the end of the three hours, I left exhausted but hopeful.

This conversation has happened to me many times. Communicating the importance of missionary discipleship as not "one more thing to do" but instead as a new way of being Church is difficult when people are exhausted and do not know any other way of being Church.

We might compare the Church to a tree. For many years, dioceses and parishes have focused on strengthening the trunk and branches of the tree. We did this by focusing on outcomes such as youth ministry and young adult ministry, for example. We believed that if we focused our efforts on a specific ministry—the branches of the tree—then the tree would be healthier. But this approach diverted energy and resources from the life of the tree, and the roots were left to wither. As a result, the trunk became weakened from the inside out, and the leaves, which should have been visible and healthy, started to decay and die.

The same is true of our lives. If we do not nourish our roots—our relationship with and love for Jesus—we will not bear fruit. Jesus tells us, "Just as the branch cannot bear fruit by itself unless it abides in the vine, neither can you unless you abide in me" (John 15:4). And similarly, "whoever does not abide in me is thrown away like a branch and withers" (John 15:6).

The root of our lives and our parish tree is discipleship. If you want healthy people and healthy ministries that bear fruit, then focus on the roots: discipleship. The roots ground the tree, drawing water and nutrients for energy and releasing this food at the right time for growth and nourishment. This is especially true when it comes to stewardship. The response of a disciple is to be a good steward of all that God has given. If you speak of stewardship only in terms of "time, talent, and treasure" and do not connect it to discipleship, it will not be rooted within the life of the parish.

Grappling with Urgency

In a conversation with Tim Glemkowski of L'Alto Catholic Institute, he remarked that "I was told by a Catholic company that the best thing a parish can do to renew itself is to present itself as a vibrant parish—meaning, of course, buy their marketing products. Thousands of parishes, this company claimed, have already become vibrant parishes by using their products and are seeing amazing renewal because of it. The only thing I could think was that, if their products are so effective, why are we seeing wide-scale abandonment of the faith by consecutive generations?"

What Tim speaks of here is grappling with an increased sense of urgency. Unless we believe that we are in a time of serious and unprecedented change, we will remain content with compliance and complacency. Louis V. Gerstner, former chairman and CEO of IBM, gave a talk on November 20, 2002, at the Harvard Business School, entitled "IBM's Transformation," and stated that "transformation of an enterprise begins with a sense of crisis and urgency. No institution will go through fundamental change unless it believes it is in deep trouble and needs to do something different to survive."

While it is tempting to look for a quick fix or a magic bullet, there isn't one. Tim warns us of this when he says, "Given the uniquely challenging dynamics of the cultural situation in which we currently find ourselves, though, something much deeper is needed than painting a veneer of vibrancy over our parish life by implementing 'best practices' from the business world."

What the pastors in that room were feeling is not uncommon, and they make a great point for us to be aware of. There is a danger that discipleship will become another buzzword instead of a way of life that transforms us into a true missionary Church. Our language must mirror the reality of what we hope for and dream of—what Pope Francis calls in *Evangelii Gaudium* the missionary option: "that is, a missionary impulse capable of transforming everything, so that the Church's customs, ways of doing things, times and schedules, language and structures can be suitably channeled for the evangelization of today's world rather than for her self-preservation" (#27).

It is not enough for us to exercise an ecclesial introspection; our reflection and learning must be inclusive, open, and welcoming, involving the entire Church. It is time for us to reject solutions that window-dress or mask the real issues and instead reclaim the fire of parish life from within by focusing on our people, who in turn will renew our structures.

We are now in the deepest waters of cultural change. Take a deep breath! I have been where you are at this moment, many times. It is overwhelming, exciting, and hopeful all at once. Because this process is multifaceted, I have a few helpful tools to share with you.

Building the Fire: Ministering through Complex Change

The process of change is not like baking a cake but like cooking a stew. The chart below outlines the ingredients that need to be present in our parish stew for change to manifest. It outlines the results or behaviors that you might expect if one of the processes is left out. I call this chart "Ministering through Complex Change," and it is based on the "Managing Complex Change" model by Dr. Mary Lippitt, founder and president of Enterprise Management, Ltd.

Guide to the Chart

Ingredients for Change. There are six ingredients or elements necessary for change: prayer, vision, gifts, inspiration, resources, and a pastoral plan. They are not the only ingredients but the main ones.

Result. When any one of the six ingredients is missing (where there is an O directly underneath the ingredient), there is a corresponding result that manifests itself as specific behaviors (exhaustion, confusion, anxiety, resistance, frustration, and false starts). Let's look at each element of change in turn and the corresponding behavior.

Prayer. As we outlined in the previous chapter, prayer is the first step in the disciple-making process. Going one step down in the chart, if prayer and reliance on the Holy Spirit are not present (where the O under prayer is represented), then people become exhausted and burn out.

Vision and Mission. Our vision and mission are to go and make disciples. Every parish will approach this differently. So, what is the vision for the change? Is it a vision capable of uniting the parish? If you don't have a strong vision, you will see confusion.

Gifts. We need people who have specific gifts, strengths, and charisms and who can move the vision forward. Are the right people in place? If you do not have people with the right gifts and strengths, they will most likely be anxious going through the process.

Inspiration. In order to move the parish forward, we need to inspire change. The parish statistics can be a great motivator to communicate urgency but also excitement about what lies ahead. How is the parish team going to inspire change? Resistance is the key behavior that people experience if they are urged to make change but are not inspired.

Resources. This means time, personnel, and space considerations. What resources are needed to move this change forward? How can we divert resources to our central mission? Without resources, there will be a high degree of frustration throughout the process.

Pastoral Plan. It is necessary to have a pastoral plan that is realistic and that concentrates on the vision and mission. It needs to be flexible and discussed regularly. If your pastoral plan is not tied to goals and strategies, it is likely that you will have a lot of false starts. False starts can create a sense of whiplash for parishioners and the parish team.

Ingredients for Change						Result
Prayer	Vision and Mission	Gifts (Strengths, Charisms)	Inspiration (Incentive)	Resources (Personnel, Financial, Space)	Pastoral Plan	Lasting Change
O	Vision	Gifts	Inspiration	Resources	Pastoral Plan	Exhaustion
Prayer	O	Gifts	Inspiration	Resources	Pastoral Plan	Confusion
Prayer	Vision	O	Inspiration	Resources	Pastoral Plan	Anxiety
Prayer	Vision	Gifts	O	Resources	Pastoral Plan	Resistance
Prayer	Vision	Gifts	Inspiration	O	Pastoral Plan	Frustration
Prayer	Vision	Gifts	Inspiration	Resources	O	False Starts

You can use this simple chart to unearth and assess what is happening at your parish and what is needed to address the change. Let's begin our next section (regarding the need for a pastoral plan) with one of my favorite quotes from Pope Francis.

Building the Fire: Concentrate on the Essential

During Pope Francis's address to the plenary assembly of the Pontifical Council for the Promotion of the New Evangelization (October 14, 2014), he called for a common commitment to a pastoral plan that recalls the essential and that is well centered on the essential, namely Jesus Christ. It is no use to be scattered in so many secondary or superfluous things, but to be concentrated on the fundamental reality, which is the encounter with Christ, with his mercy, with his love, and to love our brothers as He loved us.

We must abandon the mindset that programs create disciples. A program serves as a help, a tool, and a springboard. Having worked in adult faith formation, both at the parish and the diocesan level, I have struggled with the expectation placed on those in adult faith formation that an eight-week DVD program would effectively make disciples. It doesn't work that way. The disciples walked with Jesus for three years, shared meals with him, were present during his most difficult moments—and yet Peter still denied Jesus three times! Disciple-making is a process, often a long one requiring constant patience and abandonment to the grace of God. It is a multifaceted process requiring a multifaceted approach that must be planned for.

A well-thought-out process and vision are necessary for disciple-making. Yet, articulating a long-range pastoral plan is not something we have a lot of experience with. Consider a pastoral plan kindling for the fire. A simple way to look at the pastoral planning process is through the lens of something I call "the rule of three and three." This methodology employs three pathways to becoming a disciple-making ministry coupled with three focusing questions as follows:

Discernment. Before you undertake any evaluation, view the process in terms of discernment and imbue the entire process with ample prayer. Objectively assess your life and the parish's life, taking time to pray about where the Lord is leading you, while reflecting on the needs of the people you are serving.

Purification. Identify successes, weaknesses, and opportunities that are available to you. Identify areas for pruning so that new life can occur. Not everything we do bears fruit, so we must take the time to determine what is working and what isn't. Examine what is outdated or no longer working. Take the time to grieve, give thanks for all that was, and look at options for the future.

Reform. Simplify and streamline your life and your ministry to focus on making disciples of Jesus Christ. Abandon or reform programs and processes that are not in total alignment with this goal.

With these three principles in mind, ask the following questions. In order to form disciples in my personal life and in my ministry, what do I need to

- start doing?
- stop doing?
- keep doing?

These questions can guide us, regardless of our involvement with our parish, as we grow in our faith. From experience, I can tell you that it is far easier to figure out what we should keep doing and start doing than it is to decide what we need to stop doing. Parishes are unwilling to prune ministries that are no longer bearing fruit; they feel more comfortable keeping the existing, struggling ministry going, while adding new programs or events. As a result, all the ministries struggle because of the constant activity, and so every new ministry is placed in jeopardy before any momentum and fire can be generated. Yet, if we keep doing what we have always been doing, we are going to keep getting what we have always been getting.

There are many things that we are doing that warm hearts, but we need to look at them in a realistic and healthy way. Jesus tells us to go and make disciples, not bingo players or picnickers! And yet we sometimes spend more time planning for events and setting up tables and chairs than making disciples. Over time this causes our baptismal fire to die down. Every activity should have the goal of leading people to encounter Christ. If you are spending time on activities that do not introduce people to Christ, then you need to stop doing them.

While this may sound harsh, it will ultimately free you to put your time and effort into building a fire capable of sustaining itself beyond your wildest dreams.

—————————— TAKING ACTION ——————————

Pray as You Go (and Make Disciples)

Suscipe

Take, O Lord, and receive my entire liberty,
my memory, my understanding and my whole will.
All that I am and all that I possess, you have given me:
I surrender it all to You to be disposed of according to
　　Your will.
Give me only Your love and Your grace;
with these I will be rich enough and will desire nothing
　　more. Amen.

—St. Ignatius of Loyola

Personal Principle

Roger Enrico was an American businessman best known for being the chief executive officer of PepsiCo for many years. He was often quoted as saying that all organizations need to "beware of the tyranny of making small changes to small things; rather, make big changes to big things." If we want to move from low or medium commitment to being on fire for our faith, then we must be bold, innovative, and creative, and take risks. Revisit the three questions from the perspective of your life.

What do I need to START doing?

What do I need to KEEP doing?

What do I need to STOP doing?

Write down your answers, and take some time to pray about them and plan how to put them into action.

You can use the chapter 7 online printable, "Discern, Purify, Reform," to enhance your reflection. www.loyolapress.com/startwithjesus

Parish Priority

> A planning framework focused on fruitfulness suggests an approach to pastoral ministry that discerns what will be fruitful, what needs to be pruned, and *how* weeds will be separated from new growth.
>
> —*Living as Missionary Disciples: A Resource for Evangelization*, USCCB

Set aside two or three days to pray and plan as a parish team.

Using the chart in this chapter as a guide, decide on a couple of key initiatives and priorities that are centered on the essential. Work to find alignment so that all parish staff can see themselves in the process and give input.

At this point, an objective look at your parish data should be an essential part of figuring out the next steps. This can be daunting, but it can be a useful tool in strategizing toward possibilities and opportunities. Your data should be available from your diocesan offices or recorded at the parish.

Keep your plan simple and streamlined. At every parish meeting, revisit the goals and how they are being lived out in each person's ministry. Share successes and failures with honesty and humility.

Encourage one another and do not neglect to "meet together as is the habit of some but encouraging one another" (Hebrews 10:25).

You can use the chapter 7 online printable resource, "Discern, Purify, Reform," to enhance your reflection. www.loyolapress.com/startwithjesus

8

Start with Who and Why

In the Diocese of Green Bay, where I minister, there are 157 parishes, each with particular traditions, approaches to ministry, and customs. As I visit parishes every week, I see firsthand the danger of ignoring the unique culture of the local community and the parish expression of that community in favor of a more uniform approach that does not consider the needs of the parish. Fostering a culture of missionary discipleship is not a one-size-fits-all approach. There is no magic program or team that can be prescribed uniformly as a remedy. Parish culture is not pop culture.

Pop culture is a homogenous set of beliefs, practices, and habits that are popular or ubiquitous in society at a given time. Trends and fads tend to sweep through social media like wildfire and, just as quickly, fade into obscurity. We cannot have a pop-culture mindset or approach to our faith or our parish. Each of us is imbued with unique gifts and manifests the Holy Spirit in a unique way. Pope Francis reminds us:

> [T]he parish is not an outdated institution; precisely because it possesses great flexibility, it can assume quite different contours depending on the openness and missionary creativity of the pastor and the community. The parish is the presence of the Church in a given territory, an environment for hearing God's word, for growth

in the Christian life, for dialogue, proclamation, charitable out-reach, worship and celebration. (*Evangelii Gaudium*, #28)

Our parishes are communities of communities, and as such, those communities need to be united in a common vision and mission. This isn't a ministry popularity contest! Every activity in the parish ought to be aligned around shared cultural values and not compete with other activities. That means that we may have to make some serious shifts in how we currently operate.

Shifting into High Gear

The Church did not decline as an institution overnight but in small, gradual shifts that often went unnoticed over time. Through the years, I have noticed that people tend to point to a particular year or decade and view that period either through rose-tinted glasses or as the main problem. For example, "Oh, if only Vatican II had not happened, then we could go back to 1952 when the Church was flourishing" is a refrain I hear often in parish life. But this is an overly simplistic and not an entirely honest view. The past is what has brought us to the future. If we find ourselves twenty pounds over-weight, we know that it is not because we gained twenty pounds overnight but pound by pound. The years of decline that we are experiencing as a Church stretch back much further than the past fifty years, into the past five or six hundred years. Just as decline is a process, so, too, is inspiring and fostering a culture of lasting change—what I refer to as "bearing fruit." We can spend our time living in the past, or we can learn from its lessons and make the shifts that are needed now.

When I work with Catholic school principals, I ask them what the teachers' lounge or the music room in their school is called. They usually answer, "the teachers' lounge" and "the music room." When I ask what the public school calls these same rooms, they respond with the same answers. "Isn't this a problem?" I ask. "Shouldn't the rooms of our parishes speak to who we are as a people of faith?" The light bulb usually goes on when I ask them why the music room in their school is not named for St. Cecilia, the patron saint of music, or the teachers' lounge for St. Thomas Aquinas or some other saint who excelled in the world of academia.

When we cannot articulate who it is and what it is that we represent as a people of faith, we cannot blame people for thinking that it is okay to go "church shopping" and "church hopping." It is a problem when we cannot articulate from whom our identity comes.

Our identity as the People of God comes not from a "what" (here's what Catholics do) but a "who" (Jesus is the reason for our existence). So, where do we start? We start with the person of Jesus—the who, what, and why of our lives. Jesus is not simply what the Church teaches but whom the Church lives. At a conference in Norfolk, Virginia, in 2014, Father Cantalamessa, the preacher to the pontifical household, reminded us that "people will not accept Jesus based on the word of the Church, but they will accept the Church based on the word of Jesus." Rarely do we talk about the who or the why: introducing people to Jesus Christ and his Body, the Church, and the unique expression of who Jesus is in our lives. As Catholics, the miracle of transubstantiation is at the heart of who we are as a people of faith. And it is our baptism that has unleashed in us the grace to live as disciples of Christ. A recovery of "who" and "whose" we are is critical. This is an echo of the words of St. Augustine, who said that we should behold what we are (made in the image and likeness of God) and receive who we are (Jesus Christ).

Leading with the "who" of Jesus rather than the "what" of the Catholic Church is the first step in helping people come to a relationship with Christ, particularly at a time when institutional mistrust is high across all institutions but especially regarding the Catholic Church.

Start with Jesus. He is the reason for our existence and gave us the mandate to evangelize and make disciples.

From the Institution to a Person

We can no longer have a business-as-usual mentality when it comes to our faith and our parish. If we think we can continue to invite, welcome, and form people today the same way we have for the past half century, then we are in for a rude awakening. With new generations coming of age and entering adulthood, we are seeing more clearly how our approach needs to change. I was reminded how foreign some of our processes are to young people when I was talking with a young man recently. Joe, who is in his twenties, said to me that although he enjoys attending Mass a couple of times a year, he has not and will not join a parish. "Too many hoops to jump through" he said. "I work during the day and sometimes at night, so the parish office and church are usually closed when I think about stopping in on the way home from work."

Joe also observed that the way we collect money at Mass is in itself an outdated process and not convenient for young adults. I was curious and asked him about this. "The vast majority of young people do not carry any form of cash on their person. They are far more comfortable with forms of e-giving such as Apple Pay, and yet there is no option to give spontaneously at our parishes if we want to," he said. "Maybe putting in a Square app on an iPad at the back of the church, so that people could give if they were moved to, wouldn't be a bad idea." Now, asking a rural parish with limited technology to do this might be a difficult undertaking. But for urban parishes in areas with a high concentration of young adults, this might be a great way to communicate that the parish values young people and their gifts to the church—literal and spiritual!

From What and How to Who and Why

Explanations of the gospel from older Christians often attempt to answer questions that millennials and teens aren't asking today. Previous generations asked questions like "How do I get to heaven?" or "What do I do with my guilt?" Younger generations today ask entirely different questions like "What does it mean for me to thrive as a human being?" Teens and young adults are asking where they belong, how they are significant, how to deal with anxiety, and what to do with their loneliness. As one campus minister remarked, "If our gospel can't answer those questions, it doesn't feel like good news."

Today's world, and particularly the young people, are asking "why" questions. Why do you believe? Why should I believe? What difference could Jesus make to my life? People can search online for the answers to the "what" and "how" questions of faith, but they can learn about a lived faith only in relationship to others. Unless we come to grips with who Jesus is in our lives, the why of our faith will not be coherent.

This shift from the "what" and "how" to the "who" and "why" can be summed up as a shift from an institutional approach to faith to a Christo-centric approach. For postmodern young adults, this shift is particularly important because they have a natural skepticism of those in authority and of institutional authority in general, particularly in the wake of the sexual abuse scandals.

Let's break down the "what," "how," and "why" of parish life further by examining how we approach faith formation.

What: Faith formation opportunities so that our parishioners can grow in faith.

How: Through classes, sacramental preparation, and retreat experiences

Why: Because growing in faith and growing in relationship with Jesus Christ is an important part of being a Catholic

Let's flip this process, beginning with the "why."

Why: We believe that every person is a gift from God, who wants to grow in relationship with each person. We believe that every person can reach full potential and grow in faith.

How: We provide opportunities to grow in faith that are age appropriate, family focused, and open to the unique needs of each person.

What: We offer classes, retreats, and opportunities and experiences such as sacramental preparation and faith formation.

This process is far more attractive and compelling, especially to those seeking a parish home.

If we were to take this approach to sharing our faith and inviting people to our parishes, can you imagine how this thinking would transform us?

Start with Who: Jesus Is the Reason

One day, as my friend Jennifer and I were having a cup of tea, she asked me a great question: "What's the benefit of joining a parish, anyway?"

"What do you mean?" I asked.

"Well, I mean, what is the *actual* benefit to someone's life? I know my parish would bury me if I died," she continued, "but I don't see what the actual benefit is of joining a parish versus being a casual member and just showing up for Mass. Nobody notices whether I am there or not anyway." Ouch!

Jennifer's question gets to the heart of why we are Catholic and also why many Catholics stop coming to Mass. Often we are so concerned with the what and how of faith that we forget who is the most important: Jesus and the people we serve. People want to be noticed and loved. They want to feel that they belong—that they care for others and others care for them. St. John Bosco said that it is not enough to tell people that they are loved; people must *feel* that they are loved. How many people would say that their parish community loves them?

In *Start with Why: How Great Leaders Inspire Everyone to Take Action*, Simon Sinek argues that organizations that are continually innovating and growing begin not with "what" they have to offer but "why." As Catholics we have to live out of a "who" and "why" mentality. A simple but profound question for us to ask ourselves is "How does my life point to Jesus?" As parishes shift from maintenance to mission, they should ask "How does this activity/event/program/process point to Jesus?" These questions are transformative in that they take what is stale and rote (for example, our approach to prayer or our parish meetings) and center them on the person of Jesus.

Let's apply this thinking to how we welcome and love our potential new community members.

Step 1: We wait for them to come to us. Those who are seeking to join our community must first come to us at the parish during hours that are rarely convenient for those who work outside the home.

Step 2: We meet with them and ask them all kinds of informational questions. After a brief meeting, usually with the parish secretary, we hand them a registration form asking data-driven questions such as household size, occupations of those who live in the home, ages of those in the household, and so on.

Step 3: When they return their registration form to us, we hand them a packet of information about events and activities and Mass times. These events and programs may or may not apply to their lives, but rarely do we find out what their daily lives are like, what they need from our community, and how they might enrich our community.

Step 4: We talk about how they are going to contribute financially. We hand them a box of envelopes for their contributions to our parish or enroll them in an online giving program.

Process over.

What does this process communicate about whom our parish believes in and what is important? How does this process speak the person of Jesus to the person sitting in front of you who is a beloved child of God? If we consider our parish as a family, is this how we would welcome people to our family?

The overall perception such a process inspires is that the parish is an organization with activities and a budget. The message to the person on the other side of this process is that what we have going on at the parish is far more important than how new members are received as gifts to enrich our community by their presence, contribution, and talents. We do not communicate that our life together centers on Jesus and our primary purpose is to serve others. Rarely do we stop to ask others about their life stories or any concerns they have about which we can pray.

Furthermore, we don't seem to ask the hard questions about why people are not joining our parish or even why our process looks the way that it does. Is it any wonder that people, especially young adults, are not clamoring to join our parishes? We as a Church have largely put the "what" and the "how" before the "why."

So, let's take the example of new-member registration but approach it through *who* and *why*.

Start with who. Who is the center of our lives and our parish? Jesus Christ. Who are the people that help welcome new members? Not just the administrative assistant but the entire parish. And who is the person on the receiving end of our parish process? The potential new member. How can we shape this process around the people we have identified?

Jesus. We are encouraging people to become part of our community so that they can draw closer to Christ and to one another. Jesus Christ is at the heart of every process.

Parish team. It is not the responsibility of one person to be the entire welcoming process for the parish. All of us share in welcoming new members, inviting people we love to take a second look at our community. We are the welcoming team. On the parish staff, the administrative assistant should be the first step in a continuum of care for the new member, and those engaged with the registration process should be warm, inviting, and truly knowledgeable about what the parish can offer. We are all in this together!

Person joining the parish. This potential parish member is created by God and imbued with gifts and talents, a person seeking to be embraced, a person we want to connect with as a family of faith. What are this person's unique needs and gifts? What is her or his story of faith? What has led him or her to this moment? Why does he or she want to join this community? This kind of thinking frames the process of registration, not simply from a parish perspective, which is more programmatic, but also from a personal perspective.

We can rearrange and enhance the registration process, beginning with relationship—with *who*.

Who. Do the people who register new members at your parish love their faith? Love Jesus? Love the parish? Who on the parish team connects and follows up with new members? How is follow-up conducted? Who mentors new members?

Why. Why would someone join our parish and not another parish? Are we hoping that new members will become engaged in the work of the parish through activities and events, or do we attract them through community and relationships?

How. How is this person accompanied through the process of joining this new community of faith? How do we ensure that the process is not too arduous and difficult? How do we introduce new members to Jesus?

What. What are we truly inviting people to experience at our parish? What kind of community can people expect to encounter? What are the means by which we help people come to a deeper understanding of their faith? What does our registration process entail? More important than telling people what your parish can do for them is helping people see what gifts they bring to the parish and what their needs are.

Where. How are we hoping to reach new parishioners? Are we expecting them to come to us? Do we go out into the community? Knock on doors? Are we present at community events such as farmers markets, neighborhood celebrations, healthy living days, or kids' days to connect with new people?

When. When can people register at the parish? At a particular time of the month? At Masses? Is registration flexible or fixed? Must all of it be done in person, or can some of the paperwork be submitted online?

This kind of thinking is transformational in that it frames the process within the context of relationship—to others and to Christ.

From the Inside Out

I realize that this kind of thinking takes extra effort and time, but it is well worth it. Sinek notes that "when most organizations or people think, act or communicate, they do so from the outside in, from WHAT to WHY" (*Start with Why*, 39). But inspired leaders and organizations operate the opposite way: from the inside out. The same is true of our ongoing conversion to Jesus. Conversion is the fire of new life that transforms us on the inside and is visible to others on the outside. Discipleship is not about behavior modification but about the conversion of heart and mind, which always leads to lasting change. Our parishes will be renewed only in the same way conversion takes place: from the inside out.

— — — — — — — — — — **TAKING ACTION** — — — — — — — — — —

Pray as You Go (and Make Disciples)

My Lord God, I have no idea where I am going. I do not see the road ahead of me. I cannot know for certain where it will end. Nor do I really know myself, and the fact that I think that I am following your will does not mean that I am actually doing so. But I believe that the desire to please you does in fact please you. And I hope I have that desire in all that I am doing. I hope that I will never do anything apart from that desire. And I know that if I do this you will lead me by the right road, though I may know nothing about it. Therefore, will I trust you always, though I may seem to be lost and in the shadow of death. I will not fear, for you are ever with me, and you will never leave me to face my perils alone.

— Thomas Merton, *Thoughts in Solitude*

Personal Principle

As you assess the "soil" of your faith, revisit the parable of the sower that is outlined in the online printable resource for this chapter.

Tilling is backbreaking work and involves breaking up hardened ground, pulling weeds, and getting the soil ready for planting. Seed planting is not as labor intensive but is more focused, precise, and specific. All these processes work together to bring growth. *Explore what the growing process looks like for you using the chapter 8 online printable resource, "Sow, Grow, and Go."* www.loyolapress.com/startwithjesus

Parish Priority

> In all cases, going back to the original purpose, cause or belief will help these industries adapt. Instead of asking, "WHAT should we do to compete?" the questions must be asked, "WHY did we start doing WHAT we're doing in the first place, and WHAT can we do to bring our cause to life considering all the technologies and market opportunities available today?"
>
> —Simon Sinek, *Start with Why*, 51

When you bring various parish teams together, sometimes the conversation is marked by unhealthy competition and fear. As one parish leader said to me, "We think our parishes are growing when they are cannibalizing parishioners from other parishes if they have a more attractive Mass time or a more dynamic pastor. But when Mass times change or pastors move on, the parishioners move with them." We must revisit the essential mission and charism of the parish community so that people understand *who* and *why* are at its heart.

Most parishes have a vision and mission statement. Sometimes ministries within the parish have their individual vision and mission statements too. Collect those statements and bring them all together. Many times, these statements are posted on a wall, and after the initial excitement has worn off, few people revisit them. The culture and values that the parish community is trying to live out are not embodied in parish life.

Take another look at these statements to understand the people, culture, and values of the parish community. What culture and values are being articulated in these statements? Are they statements of what we believe and what we do or whom we believe in and why? What core beliefs or values emerge from them?

You can use the chapter 8 online printable resource, "Who, Why, What, and How: Our Parish Focus," to enhance your reflection. www.loyolapress.com/startwithjesus

9

From the Inside Out: Our People ARE the Program

The question posed by a newspaper, "What is wrong with the world?" was answered by Catholic author and writer G. K. Chesterton as follows:

"Dear Sirs:
I am.
Sincerely Yours,
G. K. Chesterton."

We the People: We the Missionary People

"I am." These two simple words continue to move us more deeply into a missionary paradigm. We often hear people state, "What is wrong with the Catholic Church is X and Y," or, "What is wrong with the parish is Y and Z." The problem with this thinking is that it is individualistic and narrow. *We*—the members of our parish communities—are often what is wrong with the Church, and it is far easier to blame a structure than to look at ourselves and our role in the parish community. We complain about the lack of hospitality at Church but then fail to welcome others to Mass or to extend ourselves to someone we don't know. We complain about others being à la carte

Catholics, yet how many of us skip over the more difficult aspects of Catholicism?

Becoming a vibrant parish is the result of small, intentional steps initiated at the parish leadership level but also accepted by each disciple personally. The preamble to the U. S. Constitution begins by emphasizing its most precious resource—its citizens—with the words "We the People." The same is true of the Catholic Church. The Church is not just buildings and ministries but the people who enliven them. If our people are renewed, our parishes will be renewed, and the world will be transformed. People are always our best resource in the disciple-making process. "We the missionary people" are the ones who will renew our parishes but only if we have been renewed by the Lord Jesus Christ himself, who wants disciples and not merely admirers.

Disciples, Not Admirers, Always Ready

In his essay "Followers, Not Admirers," Søren Kierkegaard points out that Christ "never asks for admirers, worshippers, or adherents." Christ always desires that we become his disciples. "It is not adherents of a teaching but followers of a life Christ is looking for. Christ understood that being a 'disciple' was in innermost and deepest harmony with what he said about himself. Christ claimed to *be* the way and the truth and the life [Jn. 14:6]," says Kierkegaard. Immature faith is centered on admiration; mature faith is the path of discipleship. A mature faith actively wrestles with the demands of gospel living, has a willingness to live out those demands, and invites others to share in the gospel message. *The General Directory for Catechesis* describes mature faith as "a living, explicit and fruitful confession of faith" (#82). Many times, we focus only on faithfulness as the most important attribute of a disciple's life and neglect what it means to be fruitful as a disciple. Faithfulness and fruitfulness work together in the disciple-making process. In nature, a tree is known by its fruit. In the spiritual world, a disciple's life is always marked by fruit: "These are the ones who, when they hear the word, hold it fast in an honest and good heart, and bear fruit with patient endurance" (Luke 8:15). The work of the disciple's life is always visible and concrete, evidenced by strong relationships and growing communities that move out to share and inspire others with the joy of the gospel.

Pope Francis reminds us that "being a disciple means being constantly ready to bring the love of Jesus to others, and this can happen unexpectedly and in any place: on the street, in a city square, during work, on a journey" (*Evangelii Gaudium*, #127). This can happen to us at the grocery store or on social media. I often describe missionary disciples as being "tabernacles with feet" as they bring the Word of God to the world in their daily living. The goal of parish life is to inspire, equip, and shepherd disciples and create disciple-makers who go out to disciple others. Our goal is not to create admirers of Christ who leave their faith at the door of the church. The parish ought to be a center of missionary outreach, where disciples are formed and equipped to become missionary disciples at the service of the world. If we put ministers in positions where they do not understand the disciple-making process or do not have a willingness to grow in their faith, it affects the spiritual climate of our parishes. Let me give you an analogy to help undergird this point.

When a group is hiking, the slowest person sets the pace for the group. In our parishes, the pace of change is often set by the person(s) or groups who are most resistant to change. It is this group that I often call the "C.A.V.E. Dwellers" (Consistently Against Virtually Everything) that sets the tone for the parish. This group will continue to hold back the pace of change, and it affects everyone. This has got to change. People want spiritual tour guides who accompany them on their journey, rather than travel agents who simply tell them where they should go.

The Power of Presence: From Travel Agents to Tour Guides

As we have learned, a heavy or disproportionate reliance on programs can be a serious deficiency when making disciples. The discipleship process is not a string of events and programs woven together but a process that speaks to people's deepest longings, sufferings, hopes, and dreams. Making disciples includes events and programs, but the best outcomes happen when programs are tied together by ongoing relationships, especially in the natural and spontaneous moments that life affords.

We are all asked to make an adjustment from being mere "travel agents" (dispensing information or resources) to "tour guides" (accompanying others as they move through the discipleship process), as my friend Joe often remarks. Thinking of ourselves as spiritual tour guides will help us get in the frame of mind to better accompany others through the ongoing process of conversion. As conversion happens from the inside out, transformation of our parishes happens from the inside out. Two habits that are important for us to practice, no matter where we are or what role we play, are the power of presence and the ministry of interruptions.

The power of presence creates an opportunity for us to treat each person we meet as an encounter with Christ, remembering that we too can be, for someone else, an encounter with Christ. Each person we meet should feel valued and loved. Pope Francis reminds us:

> Jesus himself is the model of this method of evangelization which brings us to the very heart of his people. How good it is for us to contemplate the closeness which he shows to everyone! If he speaks to someone, he looks into their eyes with deep love and concern:

"Jesus, looking upon him, loved him" (Mk. 10:21). (*Evangelii Gaudium*, #269)

This power of presence allows us to radiate Christ to others and to receive other people as gifts to be cherished. With mounting ministerial demands and busy schedules, the extra time it takes to receive people and to build relationships with them can feel daunting, but it is not optional. Relationship building is the foundation on which all other methods rest.

Leo Tolstoy's story "Three Questions" is one that I use to understand how valuable our presence is in the disciple-making process. The story outlines three questions that a wise king struggled with.

1. What is the right time for every action?
2. Who is the right person to be with?
3. What is the most important thing to do?

If you have not read this story, I urge you to read it for its depth of insight and wisdom as it relates to the mission of discipleship. But for the sake of brevity, the answers to the questions are as follows:

1. **What is the right time for every action?** Now. Now is the best time for any action because it is the only time we have power over.
2. **Who is the right person to be with?** The person in front of me.
3. **What is the most important thing to do?** The good that the person in front of me needs at this time.

These insights can guide us so that our presence is impactful, loving, and sensitive, just as Jesus is. If every person felt valued, loved, visible, and welcomed, think of how this could change our communities!

A story from my friend Bishop George illustrates this point perfectly. Bishop George Palliparambil is the first bishop of the Diocese of Miao in India and is a true missionary who has preached the gospel at great cost to his life. Bishop George came to visit me a few years ago, and I was excited to share with him the many books, CDs, and DVD programs for evangelization and catechesis that I have in my personal library. We shared some of our favorite works, and then he commented, "It is a wonder that, with all of these attractively packaged materials and resources, this country has difficulty forming disciples."

"What do you use to form disciples in your diocese?" I asked him with obvious curiosity. He turned to me and said, "We memorize the Creed and keep the animation of the Holy Spirit alive in our hearts." He then spoke of the signs of readiness in an individual and in a community and how the story of salvation continues to hold power for people, especially those hearing it for the first time. "It's like living in the Acts of the Apostles." He chuckled.

Bishop George is one of the most effective missionaries in the world, growing his diocese from one Christian (himself) to over ninety thousand in ten years. Does he use books and materials? Yes. But only after relationships have been built so that materials do not become a substitute for face-to-face interactions. Bishop George's testimony reminds us of the importance of being a living witness to the faith and of how transformative the core gospel message can be.

The second point that is closely related to "the power of presence" is something I call "the ministry of interruptions."

Welcoming Interruptions

Like most people, I sit down each morning and work on a to-do list for my day. At night, when I review my day, I often realize that I have not gotten all my tasks crossed off. As I am working in my office, the phone rings or someone comes to my door and says, "Can we talk?"

Right then and there, you and I have a decision to make. We can indicate that we are busy working on our tasks and close ourselves off to a potentially grace-filled conversation and, thus, a further deepening of a relationship. I've made this mistake before and bitterly regretted it. Or we can take the time to be with the person in front of us, offering our full attention.

When I review my day, I often notice that these interruptions were some of my most meaningful moments. We want to strive for a balance between being and doing, but this ministry of interruptions is a gift we ought to appreciate more. Attentive listening communicates the gift of presence.

A sister of the Missionaries of Charity gave me an incredibly insightful and helpful piece of advice that has stayed with me and helped me understand the importance of our own presence. In every situation, especially difficult ones, we have a choice to be loving and merciful. Our natural desire is to put limits on our mercy and love. Sister urged me to be even more merciful and loving than I naturally felt like being. The space between what we can and want to offer and God's desire for us to be generous, merciful, and loving stretches us beyond our comfort zone. The space between what we can give and what God calls us to give is filled with the grace of God. You will not regret approaching life this way, but you will have regrets if your day is driven by your task list rather than by the people who surround you.

Knowing ourselves and getting to know the people around us are among the most basic qualities of Christ-centered leaders. By the grace of God, the example of Jesus, and the fire of the Holy Spirit, we the missionary people will transform our parishes. In chapter 11, we'll look at a parish that started with Jesus.

_ _ _ _ _ _ _ _ _ _ _ _ **TAKING ACTION** _ _ _ _ _ _ _ _ _ _ _

Pray as You Go (and Make Disciples)

O Lord, O God,
Let me seek you in my desire,
Let me desire you in my seeking.
Let me find you by loving you,
Let me love you when I find you.

—St. Anselm

Personal Principle

Laypeople are a kind of nuclear energy in the Church on a spiritual
level. A layperson caught up with the gospel and living next to
other people can "contaminate" two others, and these two, four
others, etc. Since lay Christians number not only tens of thousands
like the clergy but hundreds of millions, they can truly play a deci-
sive role in spreading the beneficial light of the gospel in the world.
—Father Raniero Cantalamessa, Advent Sermon,
December 23, 2011

As you think about the insights you have gained so far, choose two
or three people who might be open to a discipleship relationship with
you. Work through a strategy for how you might enter such a relationship with this person.

*You can use the chapter 9 online printable resource, "Accompanying
Others in Discipleship," to enhance your reflection.*
www.loyolapress.com/startwithjesus

Parish Priority

Let's review. A disciple-making approach to leadership in the Church
incorporates the following:

1. Cultivating a deep reliance on God in prayer—for yourself, your team, and your parish

2. Preaching disciple-making homilies that focus on basic proclamation and missional sending

3. Fostering a culture of hope, healing, and hospitality

4. Investing in a few key disciples and spending ample time with them

5. Making small faith-sharing studies centered on Scripture essential to your disciple-making approach.

6. Making provision for accompaniment throughout your parish's formation opportunities

7. Praying with, celebrating with, and worshiping with key parish leaders. Attending Mass as a parish leadership team is powerful.

8. Providing ample opportunities for encounter/conversion. The sacraments are key here.

9. Cultivating and sharing stories of faith

10. Reading and discussing disciple-making books and articles as a parish team

Consider the list of ten foundational attributes of a missionary parish and work through the reflection tool together as a team.

You can use the chapter 9 online printable resource, "A Disciple-Making Approach to Leadership," to enhance your reflection. www.loyolapress.com/startwithjesus

10

Follow the Leader: Your Parish Process of Missionary Discipleship

Parish life can be compared to an orchestra. If the music we are playing sounds off key and discordant, it's because each ministry in the parish is playing from a different score or piece of music. Until everyone plays the same music in parish life, our music will continue to sound off beat, especially to young people. What do you need to lead an orchestra? You need a conductor. In the case of parish life, our conductor is Jesus. It is he who conducts the music we play in our parish communities, so let's start by looking at what music Jesus wants us to play together.

The Parish Symphony of Discipleship

As we know, activity alone is no guarantee that discipleship is happening in a parish. Parishes may have a packed calendar, but often these events and experiences are disjointed and end up becoming more of a distraction than an attraction. Everyone wants to have a vibrant parish, but vibrancy flows from spiritual growth rather than from busyness. To return to the symphony metaphor, orchestras can range from small chamber orchestras with fewer than twenty members to large symphony orchestras with more than one hundred members.

Regardless of size, a great orchestra plays beautiful music because of some shared foundational principles.

Intentionally Play Music Together

A buzzword today in the broader culture and in the Church is intentionality. For example, there are numerous blogs and websites devoted to "intentional living" or "intentional simplicity." As a Church, intentionality should be at the center of our efforts to evangelize and catechize our parishioners. Working together to form youth, young adults, and adults takes a concerted effort and a common vision. It requires an ability to transcend the silo mentality we often see among parish staff, who fall into the habit of conducting their ministries with tunnel vision, focused only on their respective areas.

When one or more staff members adopts a silo mentality, different ministries exist side by side but do not have reciprocity and integration in their vision and ministerial practices. Each ministry operates independently of the other, and there is little dialogue about true collaborative ministry practices or a shared vision. A side effect of this is the dreaded staff meeting in which people gather, report on what they are doing independently of each other, and leave to go back to their own ministries. This situation has to change. Every opportunity in the parish, including meetings—especially meetings—should have the central goal of making and growing disciples.

If the goal of our work is to create disciples of Jesus, then we must design processes that foster a culture of discipleship within the parish, including for every meeting. Having the entire parish staff and parish population onboard is *the* key to avoiding the silo mentality. Rather than thinking of each person as an independent player on a stage, think instead of an orchestra in which each person plays his or her own ministerial music. Each person is in harmony with everyone else through the overall mission and vision of the parish and the goal of making disciples. Everyone plays a different instrument, but only when the musicians share the same music and allow themselves to be conducted (by the Holy Spirit) does a symphony of beautiful music emerge.

"Alleluia" Is Our Theme Song!

While many people believe that worldwide membership in the Catholic Church is declining, the opposite is true. The Catholic Church is growing worldwide, and the number of baptized Catholics has grown at a faster rate than that of the world's population, according to the Vatican's Central Office for Church Statistics. The figures presented in the Annuario Pontificio 2018, in the Vatican yearbook, and in the *Statistical Yearbook of the Church* give detailed figures on the Church's workforce, sacramental life, dioceses, and parishes, noting that the number of baptized Catholics has continued to grow globally, from 1.27 billion in 2014 to 1.28 billion in 2015. The Catholic population is holding steady at about 17.7 percent of the global population. These figures are at odds with the depiction of a dying faith so often conjured by the media. But if the Church is growing worldwide, then why are Mass attendance rates hovering at around 24–30 percent nationally?

The problem lies in the fact that we are not making disciples. We have more programs, events, and resources than ever before, but in general there is a widespread disconnect between the teachings of the Church and the practice of the faith among Catholics, particularly when it comes to moral issues. Our problem is not one of attraction but one of retention. We cannot seem to keep Catholics engaged in the life of our parishes. In the global Church, we tend to do fairly well at attracting people to Catholicism, but we are hemorrhaging members from our parishes faster than any other denomination in the United States, according to Pew research from 2015. For every convert that comes into the American Catholic Church, six existing Catholics will leave. We have become, as one observer said to me, the Church for the "hatch, match, and dispatch." We see people, if at all, when they are hatched (baptism), when they find a match (marriage), and then when they are dispatched (funerals). Goodness gracious!

Although this is a cause for much concern, it should not lead to despair. The grace of God is always moving. As Pope St. John Paul II reminded us, "We are an Easter people, and Alleluia is our song." Let's give our parish life a tune-up so that the music we play is a tune people will never forget and that sustains them for life. We should not despair, but we should feel a sense of urgency in our mission as never before.

Orchestrate Discipleship for the Benefit of All

In his book *Growing True Disciples: New Strategies for Producing Genuine Followers of Christ* (Waterbrook, 2001), George Barna reports on extensive research conducted on congregations throughout the United States. He found a common pattern among all denominations: there were a plethora of programs offered in parishes but few intentional, systematic processes for discipleship and evangelization. When asked how they wanted to improve their discipleship programs, many church leaders said that they would develop a more clearly articulated plan or approach to discipleship focused on growth rather than on the usual benchmarks and standards. Barna asks, "What if we were to change our standards? Suppose we were to de-emphasize attendance statistics, square footage and income figures in favor of a commitment to depth and authenticity in discipleship?" (4). How would this mind-set change our planning? How will we ensure that the spiritual norm in our parishes is deep and expansive rather than shallow and limiting?

What we lack in most cases at the parish is a model of discipleship and an intentional process for making disciples. We must give attention to formation processes that

- transform Catholics from being merely consumers of religious services to being disciples sent on mission, and
- foster the disciplines of the Christian life, including prayer, study, almsgiving, fasting, and service.

If we make disciples in our parish, all our ministries will be enlivened! With that being said, I want to take a closer look at an area that is critical for parish life: the ministry of catechesis or religious education, including youth ministry. Strong youth participation, stewardship, service, and formation, it must be remembered, are all the fruits of discipleship.

The Gift of Religious Education

A shift is happening in many parishes throughout the United States, particularly in the area of religious education. I repeatedly hear from parish staff that they believe the renewed focus on evangelization is at the expense of formal teaching about the faith (called catechesis) and its place within the parish. Directors and coordinators of faith formation and religious education are finding their positions retitled, using the words evangelization or discipleship. This is undoubtedly a positive sign of the importance of these ministries working together. However, in the majority of cases, titles are changed but the essential duties are not, which continue to focus on a delivery system for catechesis that takes place largely in the classroom. This "window dressing" of catechesis does little good in the way of addressing real change, not to mention that it diminishes what is critical within the discipleship process in parish life.

We must stop relying on a catechetical methodology that empha-sizes prayerless programs as the sole means of transmitting faith and move to one that emphasizes the process of discipleship and focuses on the readiness of the individual.

Keeping It Real

"I know why many religious education programs are failing and yet why youth ministry is growing in some of those same parishes," my friend Sarah, who is a youth minister, said to me one day at a cof-fee shop. "I'm sure that some of these parishes have various factors involved, but I have found a common issue in my twelve years of being a youth minister. It's pretty simple, but we don't want to address it because it means we have to change." I urged her to tell me more. She explained that her high school students have religious education followed by optional youth ministry at her parish. The week after the tragic school shooting at Marjory Stoneman Douglas High School in Parkland, Florida, her high school students went to their religious education class filled with fear and tension. During their class, the catechist taught a lesson on "Thou shall not steal," which was a con-tinuation of their lesson from the previous week. Not once was the school shooting acknowledged by the catechist, either in prayer or in conversation.

Later, Sarah welcomed those same students for youth group. It was a full group and included students who were not regular attendees. What did they want to talk about? You can bet it was not their lesson on "Thou shall not steal" but the school shooting at Parkland. Many of the students confessed that they had waited all day to talk to Sarah in confidence about their thoughts on the shooting, many tearing up as they shared the sense of fear they live with that one day they might be a victim of such an act of violence. Like the great youth minis-ter that she is, Sarah was able to unite the gospel with their anguish.

She was able to pray with them and speak faith and hope into young hearts filled with sadness and fear.

Sarah's insight reveals an important point for us. Unless we bridge the gap between faith and life, people—and especially young people—will continue to write off religion as irrelevant and outdated. The late Reverend Billy Graham said on July 2, 1962, "I pick up the Bible in one hand, and I pick up the newspaper in the other. And I read almost the same words in the newspaper as I read in the Bible." Good preaching and good teaching should be balanced by keeping a newspaper in one hand and the Bible in the other. This helps ground our efforts in the here and now while casting an eye to the future so that we can prepare accordingly. For parents, this insight from Sarah is especially important. While we want to ensure that our children know a lot of information about their faith, it is more important for them to feel that they can trust us to share their deepest thoughts so that we can help them see their story as part of God's story.

There is a reason that Pope St. John Paul II called for a "new evangelization" and not a "new catechesis." We have more catechetical programs, materials, and resources than ever before in the history of the Church. While we must always strive to have strong, faithful, and dynamic catechesis, catechesis will not be fruitful in the life of a person unless he or she has been evangelized—that is, transformed by a relationship with Christ. It would be like handing someone a map or GPS without giving them a point of reference or telling them where they should go. They would wander all over the place, without a sense of direction or purpose. Catechesis without evangelization doesn't make any sense. Evangelization is largely concerned with introducing people to Jesus—the "who" and the focus of our work—while catechesis is largely concerned with the "why" questions of our faith. Evangelization and catechesis are the means by which the Catholic Church passes on the faith from one generation to the next. So, if evangelization is the deepest identity of the Church, you might be wondering, how does catechesis fit within the discipleship process? Here is an equation that might help:

E (Evangelization) + C (Catechesis) = D (Discipleship)

We need to be mindful of the adage "Don't put the cart before the horse" when we speak of the relationship between evangelization and catechesis. Catechesis is the "cart" behind the evangelization "horse." Evangelization aims to put people in touch with Jesus Christ, and catechesis builds on this relationship and formalizes it. This is one of the biggest shifts we can make in the parish. Both evangelization and catechesis build on each other and work together in the life of every person to bring him or her to a mature faith. This shift toward discipleship is not at the expense of catechesis but, rather, situates the catechetical process within a larger framework. Catechesis is a much richer process than intellectual formation, and it also includes liturgical, spiritual, and moral formation. However, catechesis has been separated from the process of evangelization and, as such, has come to mean classroom instruction and education. One does not replace the other.

If we don't attend to the evangelization process, catechesis will not be as effective or as fruitful. Correspondingly, if catechesis does not accompany evangelization, people will not be formed in the teachings and life of the Church and will struggle to understand what we say and do and why we believe what we believe. Catechesis, which unfolds the beauty and treasures of Church teaching, presupposes that **evangelization has already taken place.** Programs are tools and springboards in the process but should not constitute the entire process whereby we simply move from one program to another.

Our current catechetical model largely runs on a September–May framework that takes place for one hour a week in the classroom. However, discipleship is a way of life and is not bound by the constraints of time, nor even of our patience, programs, or processes! Discipleship progresses at the pace that the Holy Spirit wills as the agent of evangelization, and we either work with this reality or against it. Time is the currency of discipleship and remains a challenge for us if our presence in the lives of our faith formation students is confined to one hour a week. Finding ways to connect outside of the classroom is one of the best ways to watch for signs of readiness in helping someone grow in faith.

How evangelization and catechesis work together in the life of our parish can be difficult to grasp. For a long time, I struggled to come up with a simple chart that might help parishes bring these processes together. In the chart below, you will find outlined the process of evangelization united with a pedagogy for missionary discipleship and helpful methodologies. This information may seem overwhelming at first, but it serves as a template to orient our activities to the right stage of the process and refocus our parish activities in the appropriate way.

Putting the Puzzle of Evangelization, Catechesis, and Discipleship Together

A quick guide to the chart:

Stage. This process brings together evangelization, discipleship, and missionary discipleship. Each stage builds on the preceding one; there may be fluidity among the stages as someone moves up or down through them, depending on the level of trust.

Pope Francis's Terms. The terms I use are drawn from the overarching themes found in the pope's audiences and writings. You may also want to familiarize yourself with the "Formative Itinerary for Missionary Discipleship," which is outlined in chapter 6 of the *Aparecida Document* written by CELAM, the Latin American Episcopal Conference (of which Cardinal Bergoglio, now Pope Francis, was one of the authors). One of the main tenets of the *Aparecida Document* is a call for a continental mission, or a Church that goes out in search of ways to proclaim the gospel to all people.

Methodology. This is in no way meant to be an exhaustive list. It is a beginning of helpful methodologies that may work in each stage. It can be adapted depending on the spiritual climate of the parish and, most importantly, the readiness and capacity of the person in front of you.

Scripture. These are the Scriptures that most closely correspond to the stages outlined. For example, pre-evangelization is most closely oriented to the "Come and See" stage.

New Apologetics. During the International Congress entitled "A New Apologetics for a New Millennium," Cardinal William Levada, prefect of the Congregation for the Doctrine of the Faith, remarked on April 29, 2010, that Pope Benedict XVI took seriously the challenge of a new apologetics. A new apologetics seeks to bridge the gap between the head and the heart often found in more traditional apologetics and speaks to the longings of the heart in a contemporary way.

Stage	Pre-Evangelization	Evangelization	Discipleship	Missionary Discipleship
Pope Francis Emphasis	Encounter	Accompaniment	Community	Mission
Methodology	• Relationship building • Questions and answers • Healing • Hospitality • Service Opportunities • Financial management classes • Parenting classes • Social events • Sharing stories	• Initial or basic proclamation • Encounter with Christ • New apologetics • Witness/testimony • Gift inventories • Discernment • Small faith-sharing, introduction to prayer, Scripture, stories of the saints	• Catechesis • (initial/ post-baptismal/ continuing) • Charism discernment • Sacramental/ liturgical	• Ongoing formation • Apostolic leadership • Service for the transformation of communal life
Scripture	Come and See	Follow Me	Remain United with Me	Go and Make Disciples

As you can see from the chart above, the majority of our time is spent on activities, classes, and events that are appropriate to a more formal stage of discipleship. Yet most of our people are in the pre-evangelization stage. How many? Given that 70 percent of our parishioners are not coming to Mass on a regular basis, it is fair to note that potentially 60–80 percent of Catholic parishioners may be in the pre-evangelization stage of the discipleship process depending on the spiritual climate of your parish. So, when you are wringing your hands and wondering why this particular group of parishioners never turns up for X, Y, and Z, consider the chart above. They are not ready for what you are offering if it is a mass-produced program that does not take into account where they are in the discipleship process. Are there programs, I am often asked, that are appropriate for those in a pre-evangelization stage? Again, it depends. Alpha, which is a program centered on the kerygma that combines video presentations with hospitality and faith sharing in small groups, is a great example of a program that can be used in the context of building relationships with those in a pre-evangelization or early evangelization stage. Alpha aims to help participants explore the big questions of life in a simple and accessible manner. Programs that are more advanced, such as those that center on Scripture and salvation history, are more appropriate for those who are further along in the discipleship process. However, that is not to say that Alpha would not benefit people no matter their level of faith and participation in the parish. Everyone can benefit from a back-to-basics approach. Does this present a challenge for us? You bet! But it also represents a ripe mission field. Let's take a quick look at the parish mission field.

Tune Up the Choir: Mission On!

During a pastoral council meeting, members were discussing ways to bring new members into their parish, which was declining in membership each year. The question was asked, "How do we get all those people out there to come in here?" I couldn't help but wonder if this question (which I have heard many times) was the right question to ask. What do you notice about the language of the question and the way it is framed? When I hear this question, I am struck by two things.

1. The "us versus them" mentality
2. The movement from "out there" to "in here"

The focus is on bringing "those" people in here to worship with us. Often this question means, "How do we get those people to come to Mass?" The missionary-oriented question, on the other hand, asks something different: "How do we get all the people in here to go out there and reach others for Christ?" The emphasis is on the going out, the sending forth, and the people who are reached are our friends, our family members, and our neighbors.

A parish will often begin the discipleship process by revamping the parish mission statement. During this process (which can take up to a year), many unnoticed members will leave the Church quietly and without telling us. Is this what mission has been reduced to? A new mission statement on the wall of an office or classroom that few will remember, unless it is breathed into the life of the entire parish? Every parish needs to grapple with its capacity to evangelize and catechize people effectively. There is no one-size-fits-all approach because the mission field is slightly different in each community. What works well for one parish will not work for another. Like any orchestra, the music performed will be determined by the musicians and the musical selections. Each parish must decide on the music it will play in order to form, inform, and transform its members.

To move adults toward a deeper commitment to Christ, it is important to equip them with the tools to talk to other adults about their faith. Studies from the Pew Forum and the Center for Applied Research in the Apostolate indicate that the majority of Catholics are in the category of "medium commitment" and will remain so unless actively invited and challenged to move deeper. Moving Catholics from medium commitment to active and full commitment in the Church will be a continual challenge for us but one that is sure to pay rich dividends. Often, we overlook those who are sitting right in front of us when it comes to our discipleship efforts. In this case, the cliché "preaching to the choir" does not ring true—we must continually "tune up" the choir! And that includes ourselves. One of the principles of discipleship is that you can only lead people as deeply as you have gone yourself. The old saying is true: "You cannot pour from an empty cup." It's time to fill up so that we can pour for others! We must commit to our own growth and continue to grow in our journey of discipleship. We often become leaders in our parish because of two things: our love for our Catholic faith and our love for others. God calls us, and we respond. He leads, we follow. Jesus is the conductor. The parish is the orchestra. Our ministries (whether formal or informal) are the instruments that work together to play music. Our song is one of discipleship for the good of his people.

_ _ _ _ _ _ _ _ _ _ _ _ **TAKING ACTION** _ _ _ _ _ _ _ _ _ _

Pray as You Go (and Make Disciples)

The Disciple's Prayer

Lord Jesus, use me to carry on your mission as your servant and
disciple.
Help me to love with your heart, to carry out my work with
your hands, to be a voice for all that I say and do.
Merciful Shepherd, help me to live in your person, to share
generously in the carrying of your cross so that many
others may be saved by coming to know and love you
through my simple, faithful witness. Amen.

—adapted from Bishop Ricken's prayer of discipleship,
Diocese of Green Bay

Personal Principle

. . . the best predictor of growth in discipleship was neither church attendance nor consistent financial donations. Rather, discipleship heavily correlated to one's personal relationship with Jesus. That is, do you perceive Jesus as some distant figure or close to your life? Do you see Jesus merely as an admirable human role model or as your Lord God?

—Chris Lowney, *Everyone Leads: How to Revitalize the
Catholic Church*, 136

Spend some time checking in on your own discipleship efforts.

You can use the chapter 10 online printable resource, "The Daily Disciple," to enhance your reflection. www.loyolapress.com/startwithjesus

Parish Priority

Compile a list of all the parish committees, boards, and advisory teams and the names of the members of the committees. Be intentional about setting forth a plan for the growth of your parish committees, especially because many people are on multiple committees. Rarely do parishes have expectations for their committees other than membership with a largely reporting or advisory function. What is our plan for helping our parish committees grow in faith? How can we accompany them on their journey?

You can use the chapter 10 online printable resource, "Small-Group Discipleship," to enhance your reflection.

www.loyolapress.com/startwithjesus

11

The Parish That Started with Jesus

These past few years, my travels as an author have taken me across the country, working with people from rural, urban, inner-city, suburban, and remote parishes. The insights I have gleaned from these travels have formed many of the building blocks of this book.

However, I want to share with you a story of a parish in the Diocese of Green Bay, Wisconsin, that has been moving steadily along the path of missionary discipleship for a few years now. Most Blessed Sacrament Parish in Oshkosh gives a realistic and authentic look at missionary discipleship from the inside out. It is important for me in my role as director of parish life and evangelization for the diocese to be able to walk with and support parishes through this complex and multifaceted process, and I want you to understand the level of complexity that this effort requires from all of us. Even though our collective efforts are beginning to bear fruit in our diocese, we recognize that we are in a process of change that will take many years to reach a harvest.

Some years ago, Sister Marie Kolbe Zamora, OSF, founded a series of courses, which we call Catholic Evangelization Studies (CES) that are open to all. The aim of these courses is to provide practical tools that enable participants to craft deep habits of prayer, articulate the evangelical and ecclesial foundations for evangelization, and implement a mission-centered vision for themselves and their parishes. These principles can accommodate any parish reality.

Through CES, two parish staff from Most Blessed Sacrament Parish in Oshkosh have been trained over a period of years in this missionary paradigm. I want to share their parish story through the eyes of two staff members: Deacon Rick Hocking (business manager) and Shannon Ausloos (director of evangelization and discipleship).

Most Blessed Sacrament Parish

Most Blessed Sacrament Parish in Oshkosh describes itself as a typical American parish: focused on maintenance rather than mission, slowly losing members and disbanding committees from lack of interest. "We were characterized by the Midwest culture of being polite but not friendly," Shannon notes. "For example, shortly after I arrived at the parish, a picnic was organized to welcome me and our new pastor to the church. Aside from the few people I had already met, none of the parishioners came over to say hello. The faith life of the parish seemed similar. Surveys from parents stated that they were content with the programs even as more and more families pulled their children out because they weren't seeing results."

Underneath the surface, though, parts of the parish were stirring to new life. With prompting from the previous pastor as well as a handful of mission-driven parishioners, the church held a parish summit and created a discipleship task force to begin reinvigorating the parish in tandem with a diocesan focus on prayer called "Teach My People to Pray" and one on discipleship called "Disciples on the Way." Note that Shannon was not yet employed by the parish during this initial process but hired later, as a result of an intentional focus on missionary discipleship.

"This is where our changes began," Shannon and Deacon Rick affirm. What started with the sincere and purposeful prayer of a small group of dedicated disciples became a movement that began to stir the stagnant waters of parish life. Shannon mentions that for parishes in any stage of the discipleship process, it is necessary to "pray, a lot. God wants this change more than you do. He will show you what to do and, more importantly, when to do it. Patience is important in this process and can be very difficult."

Arising out of prayer, a discipleship task force began the hard work of addressing issues in the parish that were reinforcing an entrenched maintenance approach. Composed of a small number of disciples, this group looked at the parish with fresh eyes and began to put together an idea for a parish summit with an understanding that a "come to Jesus" conversation was needed with key parish leaders and parishioners. This parish summit was a critical moment for the parish in terms of galvanizing key leaders to make changes.

Shannon notes that the parish summit

> brought together our pastor, deacons, staff, and about fifty parishioners from a variety of demographics. A good part of the summit was to identify strengths and weaknesses. The group came up with about seventy "needs improvement" areas and everyone was given five "votes" to cast as they wished out of the seventy choices. When the top three choices became clear, the task was to establish teams to tackle each of the three items. Youth and young family engagement and creating disciples were two of the top three. The third was improved communication [with] our parishioners. The next step was taking the risk to start with a clean sheet of paper to address our top three weaknesses. We formed small teams, composed of parishioners with a parish liaison, to tackle each of the top three weaknesses.

The parish summit was not a one-time event but maintained momentum through regular touchpoints with the pastor to be sure that each team was aligned with his vision. Once small changes were addressed, momentum started building within the teams, who prayed with one another, shared life together, and were encouraged to be focused in their direction and purpose. Team updates were regularly published in the parish bulletin for accountability and transparency but also to communicate that change was happening for the better.

As a result of this parish summit, it became clear that a new position was needed within the parish: someone who would be the point person for all discipleship efforts. That person was Shannon.

Shannon quickly realized that "for us to transition into a vibrant parish, we needed an umbrella approach to evangelization and discipleship. We went from trying to make disciples in silos that weren't tied to each other (religious education, speakers, special parish events, prayer groups) to having a person responsible for interweaving disciples of all ages, walks of life, experiences, and faith journeys into one fabric that supports our mission statement." Having a person unite all the disparate groups, events, and opportunities together in the parish through the lens of discipleship continued to broaden and widen the conversation.

Throughout this process, the staff of Most Blessed Sacrament knew that they would have to prune existing initiatives and events that no longer bore fruit so that they could refocus the parish. As a result, there were things they stopped doing, things they started doing, and things they kept doing to ensure growth. Let's look at these three areas in more detail.

What Did You Stop Doing?

Applying our three vital questions to Most Blessed Sacrament Parish, Deacon Rick and Shannon shared these insights:

List three to four things that you stopped doing at your parish during this time.

Settling for good enough. Shannon states that "just because the information on a poorly designed flyer is correct or a VHS tape still works doesn't mean it's OK to use. The souls of our parishioners are worth investing in colored ink and new resources. It's not about being flashy but about offering our best to those we care about. And yes, it is about competing in the marketplace of ideas. The Church isn't outdated and irrelevant, so we shouldn't act like it is!"

Protecting lowercase "t" traditions. "When I [Shannon] arrived at the parish, I was told that there were no more sacred cows. However, some people still got upset when sacred cows started to tip over!" Shannon also notes that they retired parish traditions that the staff feared would be difficult for people to let go of, but no one seemed to notice when they disappeared.

Wasting time on things that don't produce disciples. Both Deacon Rick and Shannon felt strongly that the parish was spending time doing things that were not producing any fruit. Shannon notes, "Craft projects and things that don't intentionally help a child become a disciple of Jesus are not worth doing. Asking people to volunteer for roles they aren't gifted for and have no interest in is also counterproductive and may hurt their relationship with the Church. Instead, it's important to find out what they need next." Deacon Rick mentions that a pause was taken on all committee meetings in the parish so that the parish could focus on introducing the small faith-sharing process called Alpha to their parishioners.

It might be helpful to note that during this time, the Diocese of Green Bay had initiated required discipleship formation seminars for all parish staff. These seminars focused on an overview of the discipleship process, experiencing the salvation process in a new way, and sharing our story of faith. After the seminars, all diocesan staff, clergy, and parish staff were required to participate in Alpha to rediscover their personal relationship with Jesus Christ so that they could introduce it more credibly and enthusiastically to their parishioners.

Leading with rules and set timelines. Most Blessed Sacrament Parish decided to consciously focus on their people rather than on their programs. All the staff had to make this switch. Deacon Rick states, "When people call to ask about the sacraments, I now resist the urge to share too much information about a program or a set process that might be off-putting. Instead, I ask them questions about their experience of God and try to discern if they're ready for the sacrament they're inquiring about and how we can help them get there."

What Did You Start Doing?

Intentionally praying for the parish, the staff, and the parishioners. Most Blessed Sacrament Parish is blessed to be the location of the city-wide adoration chapel. Deacon Rick and Shannon affirm the chapel as being a spiritual powerhouse for the parish and other parishes of the area. This chapel has helped parishioners from across the city and beyond connect in prayer. Shannon notes, "One of the things that drew me to this parish was the twenty-four-hour adoration chapel. I am convinced that this is a huge source of life for our parish and for me personally. My most successful plans have been made while sitting with Jesus in the chapel. On top of that, I also discovered that Deacon Rick makes a daily walk around the church to pray for our parishioners. With a beautiful but simple prayer, he asks God to fill the pews with people who will seek him in all things."

Through the CES, students were asked to "Pray the Pews" regularly and visualize them being filled with new and returning people. *The chapter 11 online printable resource, "Praying in the Pews" has a simple format that you can use in your own parish.*

Both Shannon and Deacon Rick also note that the parish team has had to be more comfortable praying with and for one another. Deacon Rick says, "After Mass, we provide 'prayer partners' for those who want to pray with someone about a specific intention. This year we are also going to be launching an intercessory prayer group to pray specifically for our parish's efforts for evangelization and discipleship."

Asking why. Shannon says, "For every program, event, or opportunity, I would stop to ask why something had been done in the past and whether it was helping people become disciples. In fact, I have a sign on my wall with the parish mission statement on it: 'Living the Gospel, Encountering Jesus in the Eucharist, Bringing Others to Christ.' If something did not fit that mission statement, we didn't do it."

Focusing on adults. For many years, the Diocese of Green Bay has been helping parishes refocus their efforts on adult faith formation. Shannon provides this insight:

> As a coworker in the vineyard reminded me the other day, Jesus welcomed the children, but he taught the adults. I am convinced that if our adult parishioners, including our parents, were missionary disciples, we would have little need for formal religious education. Children would learn to love Jesus Christ in the same way they learn to love their family, and they'd learn the teachings of the Church through immersion. This sounds like a pipe dream, and it will take a long time to achieve this goal, but the more we make discipling adults a priority, the greater our chances of creating this culture of missionary disciples. For this reason, it is now rare for us to have an event (even a Wednesday night) where children take priority over adults. We help parents form their children, but we do not have a "drop and drive" program. If there is something going on for children, there is also something high-quality being offered for adults, and that is the primary focus of the parish.

All are welcome. Most Blessed Sacrament Parish realizes that hospitality and welcoming must be grounded in concrete and tangible efforts. Deacon Rick notes,

> Catholic parishes are great at saying that everyone is welcome, but often things are structured so that we cater to one group at a time. This model is ineffective for families and often ignores singles and couples without children. As much as possible, our events offer opportunities for people of all ages and life situations to be discipled at the same time. Sometimes this means finding a speaker that has wide audience appeal. More often, it means offering various programs or speakers at the same time so that families, single adults, and couples can arrive together and leave together. This absolutely requires offering childcare. The great thing about this model is that there is an intergenerational aspect to it that is natural and unforced. We really are all in this together, and you can sense a parish family taking shape.

What Did You Keep Doing?

Emphasizing a missionary vision and mission. Most Blessed Sacrament Parish has taken seriously Pope Francis's observation that we all are a mission, and it has taken steps to make sure that disciple making is at the heart of the parish. Deacon Rick notes that it is important to

> have a mission statement that is concise and that parishioners can remember easily. The first step in the parish summit was the facilitator asking us what our mission statement was. Nobody, including myself, could come close, although most people could give a snippet. It was one of those multi-sentence mission statements that was far too lengthy. The mission statement needs to be a constant drumbeat: in homilies, signage in the church and offices, bumper stickers, and so forth. To our former and current pastors' credit, they both have kept our mission statement in front of the people. One of the biggest mistakes we make in life in general is to think,

Well, I've told them; therefore, they know. We all need a reminder of what our direction and goals are, or we easily get off track.

The change that is happening at Most Blessed Sacrament Parish is truly inspiring. Shannon and Deacon Rick know that the work of missionary discipleship is a lengthy one requiring constant prayer and abandonment to the Holy Spirit. Their story should inspire and encourage you. As Deacon Rick says, "If we can do it, you can do it too with the power of the Holy Spirit!" The last question that I had for Deacon Rick and Shannon was to ask what one piece of advice they would give to the parishes reading this book. Shannon encourages us to "have a team of people who understand the vision and can support you when the road gets rough. There will be resistance, so a support team is crucial. They help you see that you're going in the right direction, and their enthusiasm reenergizes you when you get tired. Go to them when your battery is drained. And pray. Constant prayer."

While Most Blessed Sacrament Parish's story is still being written, I hope that this chapter serves as an inspiration and encouragement to your own efforts as a parish. Remember the mustard seed: from a tiny seed sprang the mighty tree. Each of our parishes contains the seeds of new life from which a mighty tree can grow.

_ _ _ _ _ _ _ _ _ _ _ _ **TAKING ACTION** _ _ _ _ _ _ _ _ _ _ _

Pray as You Go (and Make Disciples)

Come, Holy Spirit, fill the hearts of your faithful.
And kindle in them the fire of your love.
Send forth your Spirit and they shall be created.
And you will renew the face of the earth.

Personal Principle

It's not always going to cost money to turn a parish into a more welcoming parish. But it does take a willingness to change a lot of assumptions.

—Chris Lowney, source:
https://www.commonwealmagazine.org/why-we-need-entrepreneurial-church

As you consider the story of Most Blessed Sacrament Parish, what is new for you? What difference will this make for your learning? How might you share this learning with members of your parish?

You can use the chapter 11 online printable resource, "Praying in the Pews," to enhance your reflection. www.loyolapress.com/startwithjesus

Parish Priority

In *Evangelii Gaudium*, Pope Francis outlines seven principles of an evangelizing community. An evangelizing ministry

1. knows that the Lord has taken the first step in the evangelization process (#24)
2. is a supportive action-oriented community that patiently responds to people's real needs (#24)
3. bears fruit (#24)
4. is marked by deep joy and rejoicing (#24)
5. is marked by flexibility and frequent contact with its members (#28)
6. fosters a Spirit-filled environment in which members are trained to be evangelizers (#28)
7. is bold and creative in assessing how it operates and conducts itself (#33)

What is one transferable idea that you could implement from Most Blessed Sacrament Parish's experience? How will you implement this idea? What is your time line? Who is responsible for implementing this idea? How will follow-up be conducted?

You can use the chapter 11 online printable resource, "The Parish That Started with Jesus," to enhance your reflection.

www.loyolapress.com/startwithjesus

12

It Also Starts with You!

Missionary discipleship is more than a passing fad or trend in the Church. It's here to stay! Amid the crises of clerical sexual abuse, declining numbers, and aging personnel, at the heart of this call to missionary discipleship is a call to reorient ourselves to the person of Jesus and the call to holiness. Behind the numbers lies the heartbreak of parents, grandparents, spouses, friends, and children who lament those who have drifted away from the regular practice of their faith. Every single one of us has an experience of someone we love who has turned his or her back on the Catholic faith, for a time or maybe even permanently.

For me, it is my brother. He stopped practicing his faith after our mother passed away from cancer at the age of fifty-four. Filled with anger, he challenged me repeatedly about the futility of having faith "in a God who would let our mother suffer and die." Even though I have extensive training in knowing what to say, in the face of my brother's grief, words failed me. I prayed for him every day, and I prayed that we would have an opportunity to have a real dialogue about our beliefs. One day it happened.

About a year after our mother's death, he posted an image on Facebook that took my breath away. It was an image of a young man sitting at the end of a bench with Jesus sitting on the other end. It looked like Jesus and the young man were having a sensitive conversation. I prayed about how to approach what seemed to be a breakthrough with my brother; I had no idea why he posted that image or what was going on in his heart. After imploring the Holy Spirit to give me ears to hear and the right words to say, I called him with my heart in my mouth. "I saw the image you posted on Facebook," I said to him. "Oh, I had a feeling that you would give me a call," he said. He sounded tense but open. Taking a deep breath, I found the strength to say to him, "You know that space on the bench between you and Jesus?" "Yeah." "That's where our mother sits, Ian. She is holding your hand and the hand of Jesus, too."

And with that we cried. It was a beginning, a small but significant one. The beginning of a movement for my brother to consider faith and all the good that it holds for each one of us. The beginning of his journey home, I hope and pray.

As good as our parishes can be to welcome, invite, include, and disciple people, it is in our homes and neighborhoods that the vast majority of opportunities emerge in which we can grow in our discipleship efforts. First things first: the call to missionary discipleship is for you and me, regardless of where we work or where we go. Each of us must be ready to be a credible and authentic witness in the world. It doesn't mean that we will be perfect or do everything right, but with prayer and preparation we will be well equipped to share our faith with this and the next generation of Catholics. One-on-one formation can happen in our workplaces, in our homes, and on the streets.

With that being said, let's review Jesus' methodology (which we covered earlier in chapter 3) but couple it with what we can personally do to model Jesus' method with others. This brings together many elements of the last couple of chapters.

Formed One-on-One and Sent Out Two-by-Two

The small community of disciples that Jesus formed was the beginning of the Catholic Church. Jesus invested deeply in a small group of disciples and encouraged his disciples to do the same (see Matthew 28:18–19 and 2 Timothy 2:2) so that our Church would continue to grow and flourish, person-by-person, person-to-person. This next section outlines what Jesus did and offers a series of reflection questions for you in relation to your own ministry.

1. **Prayer.** Jesus prayed about whom he would choose.

   How am I praying for disciples in my ministry?

2. **Call.** Jesus called the disciples by name.

   Who am I choosing in my ministry as leaders?

3. **Healing.** Jesus healed their wounds.

   What are the wounds of these leaders? How can I facilitate the healing process?

4. **Proclamation.** Jesus proclaimed the kerygma in word and deed.

   How am I proclaiming the kerygma in my ministry? In what ways does this concretely happen?

5. **Friendship.** Jesus spent time with his disciples.

   Who do I spend most of my time with? Who should I be spending more time with for the sake of the mission?

6. **Charisms (spiritual gifts).** Jesus helped the disciples understand their charisms.

   Do I understand my charisms? How do I help others understand their charisms and how to use them?

7. **Witness.** Jesus showed the disciples what to do (healing, proclaiming, teaching).

How do I witness to Jesus in my ministry? How do I model to or apprentice my leaders?

8. **Teaching.** He taught them in word and deed.

   How is teaching part of my ministry? To my leaders? To the wider community?

9. **Formation.** Jesus equipped them for mission (to do what he did).

   Do I have a plan for my own formation? The formation of my leaders? How do I train my leaders to share the gospel and do what Jesus did?

10. **Ongoing presence.** Jesus promised to remain united in prayer and worship with the disciples through his real presence in the Eucharist, the sacraments, and the Church.

    How am I present to my leaders? Do we attend Mass together? How do I help them be part of the sacramental life of the Church? How am I part of the sacramental life of the Church?

If we wish to raise up a generation of disciples to equip the next generation of saints, we would do well to be attentive to the spiritual law of causality outlined in the *The Soul of the Apostolate* by Dom Jean-Baptiste Chautard, O.C.S.O.

> If the teacher is a saint (the saying goes) the people will be fervent; if the teacher is fervent, the people will be pious; if the teacher is pious, the people will at least be decent. But if the teacher is only decent, the people will be godless. The spiritual generation is always one degree less intense in its life than those who beget it in Christ.

In order to maximize our spiritual intensity, we must be willing to do what Jesus would have us do for him, just as he taught his disciples to do. As you consider the list above, you may notice familiar areas for growth. In prayer, ask Jesus to send you opportunities to practice in these areas so that you can shape and equip others to do as Jesus did. Seek out leaders who are gifted in areas that you are not and ask them to share their insights and wisdom. Focusing on your own spiritual health so that you can be a source of light for others is necessary for the discipleship process. Taking some advice from Pope Francis, let's look at a few things that are important for your spiritual health as a disciple no matter your role in the parish or outside of it.

The Doctor Is in the House: Fifteen Diseases and Their Cures

On December 22, 2014, Pope Francis reminded those who work in the Curia at the Vatican.

> The Curia—like the Church—cannot live without a vital, personal, authentic and solid relationship with Christ. A member of the Curia who is not daily nourished by that Food will become a bureaucrat (a formalist, a functionalist, a mere employee): a branch which withers, slowly dies and is then cast off.

So it is for us: we must remain connected to the vine because without Jesus we can do nothing. Pope Francis then went on to list fifteen diseases or temptations of the spiritual life for all Christians but especially for those who work in ministry. I have also listed the cure for each disease based on Pope Francis's words.

Disease	Cure
Feeling immortal, essential, or indispensable. Those who place themselves above others in their quest for power.	Seeing ourselves for who we are, as sinners in need of the grace of God
The "Martha Complex" or disease of excessive activity and busyness	Rest, especially by spending time with family and friends
Mental and spiritual petrification. Those who would rather spend time with paper than people and have a heart of stone for the needs of others.	Practicing humility, detachment, generosity, and unselfishness

Disease	Cure
Over-planning and functionalism. Those who would seek to plan out everything and who try to control the direction of the Holy Spirit.	Abandonment to the Holy Spirit
Poor coordination. Those who do not function harmoniously as a team and thus create scandal and disunity.	Working together in true spiritual fellowship and communion with others
Spiritual Alzheimer's. Those who have lost the memory of their personal salvation history.	Encounters with the Lord, who renews and sustains us
Rivalry and vainglory. Those who value appearances and titles over others.	Humility and seeking to put the needs of others above our own needs
Existential schizophrenia. Those who live a double life filled with hypocrisy and a spiritual emptiness, preferring to occupy themselves with bureaucracy rather than people.	Conversion
Gossip and backbiting. Those who sow seeds of discord in conversation or who attack others rather than having the courage to speak honestly and directly with those they speak of.	Honest, open, and clear dialogue
Deifying the leaders. Those who selfishly court the opinion of their leaders and who are careerists and opportunists.	Honoring God above all others
Indifference to others. Those who think only of themselves and lose the warmth and sincerity of human relationships.	Taking joy in helping and encouraging others
The funeral face. Those who treat others, especially those they consider beneath them, with rigor, brusqueness, and arrogance.	Cultivating a joyful, humorous, and self-deprecating spirit that radiates infectious joy
Hoarding. Those who focus on the consumption and accumulation of material goods.	Divesting ourselves of the need to accumulate excessive material goods and instead traveling lightly through life
Closed circles. Those who wish to belong to a circle or clique more than belonging to the Body of Christ.	Unity in Christ
Worldly profit and exhibitionism. Those who turn service into power and power into a commodity to gain greater power.	Justice and transparency for all people.

As you can see, this list is searing for all of us as we take a deeper look at our motivations and intentions. According to Pope Francis, these temptations or diseases can be truly healed only by the Holy Spirit. He also states that daily prayer; reception of the sacraments, particularly the Eucharist and reconciliation; daily contact with the Word of God; and a spirituality that translates into lived charity are vital nourishment for all of us. In addition, I would add one more practice that I believe is essential: spiritual companioning or spiritual direction.

The online printable resource that corresponds with this chapter takes these fifteen diseases as an examination of conscience so that you can pray about your motivations and be aware of any unhealthy practices in your life that you should bring to prayer.

Spiritual Direction

"Will you be my spiritual director?" Father Jim asked me over the phone. "Oh no, I am certainly not qualified as a spiritual director," I said, "but if you are open to meeting as two friends growing in faith and sharing the gospel with each other, I would be delighted to walk with you." We began meeting regularly as growing disciples and spiritual companions. Through these years, his presence in my life has been a gift and a blessing. If you do not have a spiritual companion or spiritual director, it is important that you consider finding someone with whom you can enter a relationship that will nourish your discipleship.

Why should you consider spiritual direction?

Spiritual direction is first and foremost a way for you to grow closer to God. Because God communicates with each person uniquely, it often helps to have another person to talk with about how you experience God. Spiritual direction provides an opportunity to notice, reflect on, discern, and discover where God is present in the life of each person. The subject matter of spiritual direction is whatever is happening in your life. It often includes exploring work, prayer, and relationships. It includes talking through a major life decision or cultivating a day-to-day awareness of how God is moving in your life. The spiritual director/companion practices deep listening and evocative questioning, offers support, and creates a hospitable space where you can openly and prayerfully explore where God's spirit is leading.

Spiritual directors receive formal training in the disciplines of the spiritual life and have a deep commitment to ongoing spiritual formation and growth, both personally and for those they companion. In the case of Father Jim, his years of experience, his spirituality, his love for Jesus, and our "fit" were the determining factors for me in choosing to enter such a relationship with him. Father Jim is one of the greatest treasures in my life. His very presence "speaks Jesus" to me. His disciple-making leadership has helped me grow as a disciple and disciple-making leader.

As we look at our parishes and begin to identify the most faithful, coachable, dependable, and available persons capable of growing in the life of discipleship, it is important to remember that as we lead for Jesus, we must be attentive to our own leadership style. The first person that we lead is ourselves, and while we teach to what we know, we also "attract who we are." It is imperative that we think about our own leadership style and how we accompany others.

Walk This Way: Walking the Talk

In 2018, at the Chrism Mass on Holy Thursday, Pope Francis outlined three approaches for priests that apply equally to us, "A priest who is close to his people walks among them with the closeness and tenderness of a good shepherd; in shepherding them, he goes at times before them, at times remains in their midst and at other times walks behind them." To remain close to the people, we must

- walk behind the people.
- walk among the people.
- walk ahead of the people.

While the metaphor of Jesus as the Good Shepherd is well documented in terms of theology and Scripture, I want to anchor this metaphor in the experience of a real-life shepherd. My friend Matthew is a sheep farmer in Ireland, and we chatted about how he leads his own flock of about forty-five sheep. His experience helped me see the wisdom and inherent practicality in Pope Francis's suggestions about leadership.

Every morning Matthew goes out to visit the sheep in his field. He often needs to move them from one pasture to another, and as he rounds them up, he gently pushes them as he walks with them from behind so that they know where to go.

Once he has them in place, he then moves through the herd, noticing who might be sick or lame, who might need to be clipped sooner than the others, or who seems particularly happy and content.

In the evening, he moves them to another pasture across a road, and so, using his sheep dogs to round up the sheep from behind, he steps onto the road so that he can watch for oncoming traffic and dangers. He often turns to the sheep and says "Whoa" to steady and calm them.

As disciples and leaders, we must model all three of these behaviors in our leadership style.

- **Walking behind the people.** Sometimes our people need a gentle nudge to get them moving so that they can make progress.

- **Walking among the people.** The bulk of our time should be spent in walking in the midst of people, noticing who might need a helping hand or a gentle word of encouragement. This is practicing the art of accompaniment.

- **Walking in front of the people.** We must be prepared to walk ahead to scout out anything that might be a harm or a hinderance to those we love. In this way, we can help anticipate issues that arise in the culture about which we should be vigilant or trends that develop which we can baptize for Christ.

As you consider these three modes of interacting, ask yourself which methods you employ in speaking about your faith and how you can become more well-rounded.

My last piece of advice as you grow as a disciple and help others grow also draws from the world of nature: the planting of tulips, my favorite flowers.

Planting Tulips: Darkness, Time, and Growth

When I first moved to Wisconsin in September 2001, I had no idea what lay ahead of me in terms of the famous "frozen tundra" winters. But, knowing that I would be living in the United States for a couple of years, I decided to plant some tulips so that they would bloom in the spring and remind me of home.

Consulting my neighbor, I asked her when I should plant my tulips. "Before the first frost," she told me. "When is that?" I asked. "To be safe, you should have them planted by the first week or two of October," she said. And so, I planted them in the middle of October, when mornings were growing colder and my breath was visible in the air. As I looked out at a particularly bad snowstorm in January, with temperatures that plummeted to minus-forty-degree wind chill, I had little hope that my tulips would make it.

During the month of April, when the snow had melted, I looked in vain for my tulips but saw nothing. I chalked up the experience to a harsh winter and overly optimistic advice. I resolved to plant something hardier the following year.

And then, one day I saw it! A single tulip pushing up from the ground, or, to use an Irish expression, "ag borodh," which means quivering forth. During the next few days, one tulip became twenty, and I realized that my tulips had made it!

As I reflected on this experience later, I realized that my tulips didn't suddenly pop up but had been growing all the time. They didn't shoot up on a random day in early May but had been working their way up to the light from the darkness.

In the darkness of the earth, bulbs and seeds of life are growing fervently without us ever knowing it. We think that spring is the time of new life, but the secret work of winter is always spring. The same can be said of our spiritual lives.

It is often in the dark, unnoticed winter of our heart that the spring of conversion occurs. Like the seed emerging from the depths of winter earth, conversion is a painful process of breaking through. Sometimes, when we consider those in our parish or our religious education classes, we look out with January eyes and forget that the seed of life is growing unseen in the darkness of their lives. We become frustrated that the seeds we planted are not popping up, forgetting that time, patience, and painful growth are happening without our being aware of it. One day we may get to see the bright green shoots of new life, but we should never lose hope that the slow work of the Holy Spirit is happening. The seed that dies becomes the bread of life that nourishes the whole world. Jesus tells us this himself: "Very truly, I tell you, unless a grain of wheat falls into the earth and dies, it remains just a single grain; but if it dies, it bears much fruit" (John 12:24).

New life is happening everywhere, in our own hearts and in our parishes. Often this growth happens in winter because we hold the promise of spring and new life in our hearts. If you are facing a winter in your parish, hold on to the hope and promise of the spring, which surely will come as we all grow as disciples of Jesus.

_ _ _ _ _ _ _ _ _ _ _ _ TAKING ACTION _ _ _ _ _ _ _ _ _ _ _

Pray as You Go (and Make Disciples)

Father,
I abandon myself into your hands;
do with me what you will.
Whatever you may do, I thank you:
I am ready for all, I accept all.
Into your hands I commend my soul:
I offer it to you with all the love of my heart,
for I love you, Lord, and so need to give myself,
to surrender myself into your hands without reserve,
and with boundless confidence,
for you are my Father. Amen.

—adapted from the Prayer of Abandonment by
Brother Charles Foucauld

Personal Principle

Reflect on the quote below:

In particular, two temptations can be cited which they have not always known how to avoid: the temptation of being so strongly interested in Church services and tasks that some fail to become actively engaged in their responsibilities in the professional, social, cultural and political world; and the temptation of legitimizing the unwarranted separation of faith from life, that is, a separation of the Gospel's acceptance from the actual living of the Gospel in various situations in the world.

—*Christifidelis Laici*, 2

You can use the chapter 12 online printable resource, "The 15 Diseases," to enhance your reflection. www.loyolapress.com/startwithjesus

Parish Priority

Reflect on the following quote:

Jesus means in Hebrew: "God saves." At the annunciation, the angel Gabriel gave him the name Jesus as his proper name, which expresses both his identity and his mission. Since God alone can forgive sins, it is God who, in Jesus his eternal Son made man, "will save his people from their sins." in Jesus, God recapitulates all of his history of salvation on behalf of men.

—*Catechism of the Catholic Church*, #430

You can use the chapter 12 online printable resource, "Parish Challenge," to enhance your reflection time.
www.loyolapress.com/startwithjesus

Conclusion: Let's Get Moving for Jesus!

I am still not entirely sure how it happened, but over the July 4 weekend in 2017 I found myself in Orlando, Florida, welcoming more than 3,500 leaders to the Convocation of Catholic Leaders on behalf of the USCCB. This entire event was livestreamed and televised on EWTN. It was the most terrifying, overwhelming, and, at the same time, profoundly moving experience of my life. I was delighted and humbled to act as co-emcee for the event along with Bishop Edward Burns of Dallas and Gloria Purvis of EWTN. This event was the response of the Catholic Church in the United States to Pope Francis's apostolic exhortation *Evangelii Gaudium*.

The last time the USCCB held such a gathering was in 1917, so you could say that this event was a hundred years in the making! The convocation brought together leaders from apostolates, parishes, dioceses, ministries, colleges, and universities from Maine to the Marshall Islands and everywhere in between. And it was certainly joyful. But, far from being an event for a select group of people, the convocation was aimed at invigorating the Catholic Church in the United States by moving us into a missionary landscape.

A national moment of unity, the convocation was a clarion call for us to become missionary disciples who, nourished by our conviction of the gospel message and the love of God the Father, rush from our parishes and homes to share this Good News with the world. At the convocation, we were reminded that we don't have a mission; we *are* a mission. Each of us has been created in the image and likeness of God and acts as a unique witness to the gospel, inside and outside our parishes. Our parishes must become centers of missionary outreach because the reality is that they continue to be the primary experience of Church for many people. Parishes are without a doubt the "most important locus in which the Christian community is formed and expressed," according to the *General Directory for Catechesis* (#257). We are all challenged to find ways to effectively reach those who do not have a faith home, do not attend Church regularly, or do not have a strong parish connection. Thus, there is a direct relationship between the vibrancy of the local parish and its ability to foster growth in discipleship among its adults. It is safe to say that *the more vibrant the faith life of the local parish, the more effective it will be in nurturing mature discipleship among its adult members.* It also follows that the more contact and involvement adults maintain with their parish, the more likely it is that they will continue to grow in discipleship.

During the convocation, I had shared a story from my own life that I thought would be inspiring to the delegates. One Sunday at Mass, as my family was going up to receive the Eucharist, my son Ian, who was three at the time and quite impatient with the pace of those receiving Eucharist, shouted out at the top of his voice, "Come on, everybody, get movin' for Jesus!" As you can imagine, this outburst garnered quite a chuckle from the parishioners, while his parents were slightly mortified!

At the end of the closing Mass of the convocation, the papal nuncio, Archbishop Christophe Pierre, gave a report on the event that he was preparing for Pope Francis.

Closing the convocation, he stated that he would not be ending with a quote from a pope, an archbishop, or a document but instead—fittingly—with the words of a child. You can imagine my surprise when he ended the convocation with an exhortation for the Catholic Church in the United States to get out and get moving. Yes, the Convocation of Catholic Leaders concluded with the words of my son: "Come on, everyone, it's time to get moving for Jesus!" And so too will this book.

There is no better time than now to reclaim the fire of your faith. This is the moment. This is our time. This is the day to reclaim the fire of parish life.

Come on, parishes, come on, everyone, let's get movin' for Jesus!

About the Author

Julianne Stanz is a nationally known speaker, retreat leader, storyteller, and the Director of Parish Life and Evangelization for the Diocese of Green Bay and a consultant to the USCCB Committee on Catechesis and Evangelization.